NetApp®

Go further, faster

Technical Report

NetApp and VMware vSphere Storage Best Practices

Vaughan Stewart, Larry Touchette,
Mike Slisinger, Peter Learmonth, NetApp
Trey Layton, Cisco
July 2010 | TR-3749 | Version 2.1

ISBN: 978-0-557-09451-6

TABLE OF CONTENTS

1 INTRODUCTION

 NetApp
Go further, faster

Storage Administrators

vmware

VI Administrators

CISCO

Network Administrators

APP OS

Virtual Machine Configuration Administrators

1.1 EXECUTIVE SUMMARY

NetApp[®] technology enables companies to extend their virtual infrastructures to include the benefits of advanced storage virtualization. Our unified storage platforms provide industry-leading technologies in the areas of storage efficiencies, instantaneous VM and datastore cloning for virtual servers and virtual desktops, and virtual data center backup and business continuance solutions.

This technical report reviews the best practices for implementing VMware[®] vSphere™ with NetApp unified storage arrays. NetApp has been providing advanced storage features to VMware solutions since 2001. During this time, NetApp has developed operational guidelines for storage arrays running Data ONTAP[®] and ESX/ESXi Server. These techniques have been documented and are referred to as "best practices." This technical report describes them.

1.2 IMPLEMENTING BEST PRACTICES

The recommendations and practices presented in this document should be considered deployment requirements unless otherwise stated. While not implementing all of the contained best practices does not affect your ability to obtain support from NetApp and VMware; note that disregarding any of these practices commonly results in the need to implement them at a later date, on a much larger environment, and often with the requirement of application downtime. For these reasons we advocate that you implement all of the best practices as defined within this document as a part of your initial deployment or migration.

All recommendations in this document apply specifically to deploying vSphere on NetApp. As such, the contents of this document supersede all recommendations and best practices expressed in other NetApp documents.

Note: Data ONTAP version 7.3.1.1 or later is required to implement the NetApp vSphere plug-ins. If you plan to run an older version of Data ONTAP, you may need to use manual process to apply some of the configuration changes described in this document.

In addition to this document, NetApp and our partners offer professional services to architect and deploy the designs contained within this document. These services can be an attractive means to enable optimal virtual storage architecture for your virtual data center.

1.3 INTENDED AUDIENCE

This best practice document is part of the NetApp Technical Library and is intended for use by individuals responsible for architecting, designing, managing, and supporting VMware Virtual Infrastructures. Readers of this content should, at a minimum, be familiar with concepts pertaining to VMware ESX/ESXi Server 4.0, vCenter™ Server 4.0, and NetApp Data ONTAP 7G.

We have identified the following roles of individuals who will find the content in this document useful and each section will begin with identifying the administrative team required to implement the technology and/or configurations presented within.

2 AN OVERVIEW OF VMWARE STORAGE OPTIONS

This section applies to:

Storage Administrators

VI Administrators

2.1 AN INTRODUCTION TO STORAGE IN A VIRTUAL INFRASTRUCTURE

VMware ESX supports three types of storage configurations when connecting to shared storage arrays: VMFS datastores, NAS datastores, and raw device mappings. It is assumed that customers understand that shared storage is required to enable high-value VMware features such as HA, DRS, VMotion™, and fault tolerance. The goal of the following sections is to provide customers information to consider when designing their virtual data center.

VMware virtualization technology makes it easy for customers to leverage all of these storage designs at any time or simultaneously. The following section reviews these storage options and summarizes the unique characteristics of each technology within a virtual architecture.

2.2 THE VALUE OF MULTIPROTOCOL STORAGE ARRAYS

The virtualization of a data center results in physical systems being virtualized as part of a cost savings effort to reduce both capex and opex through infrastructure consolidation and increased operational efficiencies. These efforts result in multiple VMs sharing physical resources, including shared storage pools known as datastores. Virtualizing demanding, business-critical applications such as e-mail or database servers makes gains in operational efficiencies. This latter group of systems might share server resources but is typically configured with exclusive access to the storage it requires.

VMware and NetApp both offer technologies that natively support multiple storage protocols. These technologies allow customers to deploy best-in-class virtual data centers that leverage the strengths inherent when using these technologies together. This is not a mere discussion of SAN versus NAS basis, but rather a consideration of the operational value based on the type of storage network interconnect available to a virtual data center.

Whether your storage network is Fibre Channel (FC) or Ethernet (NFS, iSCSI, and FCoE), these technologies combine with NetApp storage to scale simply the largest consolidation efforts and virtualize the most demanding applications without sacrifice or the need to deploy separate hardware to meet the needs of either environment, this is virtualization, and it is what's valuable in a storage array platform.

2.3 THE 80/20 RULE

In designing the storage architecture for a virtual data center, you can apply what we refer to as the 80/20 rule, which is that 80% of all systems virtualized are for consolidation efforts. The remaining 20% of the systems are classified as business-critical applications, and while these can be virtualized successfully, they tend to be deployed on shared storage pools but in what we refer to as isolated datasets.

THE CHARACTERISTICS OF CONSOLIDATION DATASETS

- VMs that do not require application-specific backup and restore agents.
- The largest dataset in terms of number of VMs and potentially the total amount of storage addressed.
- Individually, each VM might not address a large dataset or have demanding IOP requirements, yet the collective whole might be considerable.
- These datasets are ideally served by large, shared, policy-driven storage pools (or datastores).

THE CHARACTERISTICS OF ISOLATED DATASETS (FOR BUSINESS-CRITICAL APPLICATIONS)

- VMs that require application-specific backup and restore agents.
- Each individual VM might address a large amount of storage and/or have high I/O requirements.
- Storage design and planning apply, as it did with physical servers.
- These datasets are ideally served by individual, high-performing, nonshared datastores.

Consolidated datasets work well with NFS datastores as this design provides greater flexibility in terms of capacity and flexibility than SAN datastores when managing hundreds or thousands of VMs. Isolated datasets run well on all storage protocols; however, some tools or applications might have restrictions around compatibility with NFS and/or VMFS.

Unless you are globally unique, the evolution of your data center from physical to virtual will follow the 80/20 rule, and the native multiprotocol capabilities of NetApp and VMware will allow you to virtualize more systems more quickly and more simply than you could with a traditional storage array platform.

2.4 VMFS DATASTORES

The VMware Virtual Machine File System (VMFS) is a high-performance clustered file system that provides datastores, which are shared storage pools. VMFS datastores can be configured with LUNs accessed by Fibre Channel, iSCSI, or Fibre Channel over Ethernet. VMFS allows traditional LUNs to be accessed simultaneously by every ESX server in a cluster.

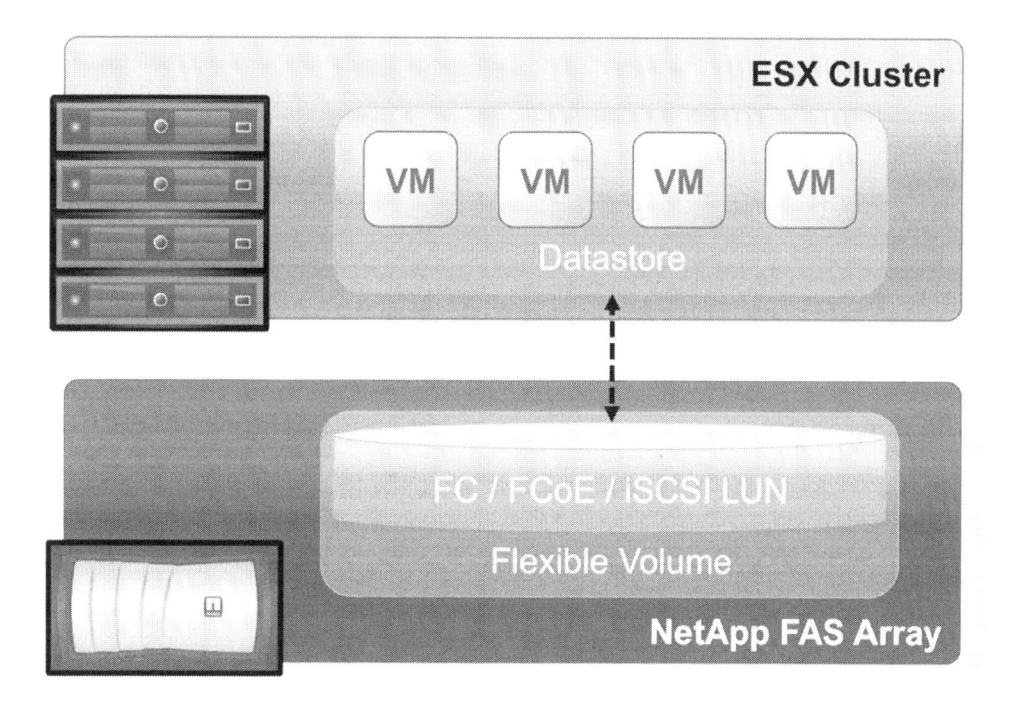

Figure 1) ESX cluster connected to a VMFS datastore using FC, FCoE, or iSCSI LUNs.

VMFS provides the VMware administrator with a fair amount of independence from the storage administrator. By deploying shared datastores, the VMware administrator is free to provision storage to virtual machines as needed. In this design, most data management operations are performed exclusively through VMware vCenter Server.

Applications that traditionally require storage considerations in order to make sure their performance can be virtualized and served by VMFS. With these types of deployments, it is recommended to deploy the virtual disks on a datastore that is connected to all nodes in a cluster but is only accessed by a single VM.

This storage design can be challenging in the area of performance monitoring and scaling. Because shared datastores serve the aggregated I/O demands of multiple VMs, this architecture doesn't natively allow a storage array to identify the I/O load generated by an individual VM.

SPANNED VMFS DATASTORES

VMware provides the ability of VMFS extents in order to concatenate multiple LUNs into a single logical datastore, which is referred to as a spanned datastore. While spanned datastores can overcome the 2TB LUN size limit, they are most commonly used to overcome scaling limits imposed by storage arrays that use per LUN I/O queues. These traditional architectures place a limit on the number of simultaneous commands that can be sent to a LUN at a given time, which can impede overall I/O performance in a datastore.

Storage arrays powered by Data ONTAP are free of this legacy architecture, and as such NetApp does not recommend the use of spanned VMFS datastores.

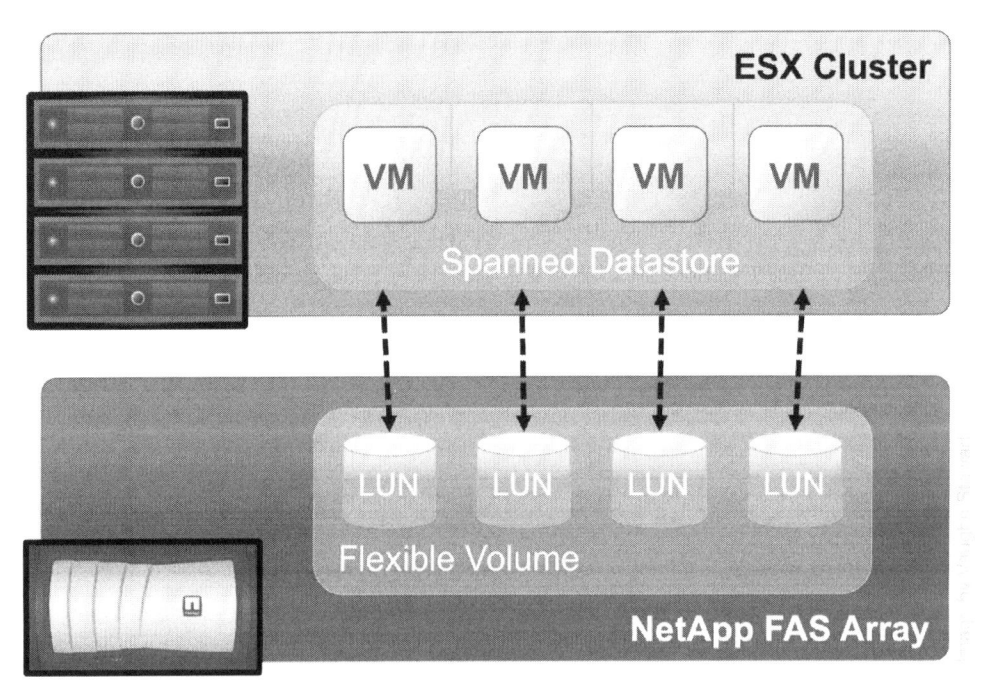

Figure 2) ESX cluster connected to a spanned VMFS datastore.

VMFS DATASTORES ON NETAPP LUNS

NetApp enhances the use of VMFS datastores through many technologies, including array-based thin provisioning; production-use data deduplication; immediate zero-cost datastore clones; and integrated tools such as Site Recovery Manager, SnapManager[®] for Virtual Infrastructure, the Rapid Cloning Utility, the Virtual Storage Console, and SANscreen[®] VM Insight. Our queue depth free LUN architecture allows VMFS datastores to scale greater than with traditional array architectures in a natively simple manner.

2.5 NFS DATASTORES

vSphere allows customer to leverage enterprise-class NFS arrays in order to provide datastores with concurrent access by all of the nodes in an ESX cluster. This method of access is very similar to that with VMFS. NetApp's NFS provides high performance, the lowest per-port storage costs, and some advanced data management capabilities.

Figure 3 displays an example of this configuration. Note that the storage layout appears much like that of a VMFS datastore, yet each virtual disk file has its own I/O queue directly managed by the NetApp FAS system.

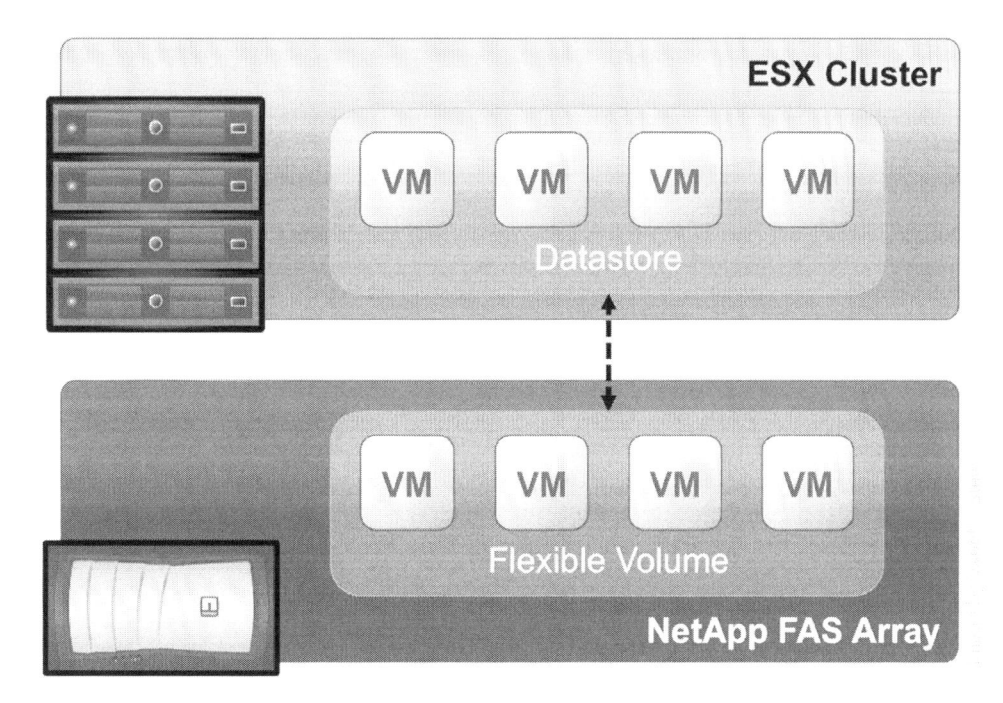

Figure 3) ESX cluster connected to an NFS datastore.

NFS DATASTORES ON NETAPP

Deploying VMware with NetApp's advanced NFS results in a high-performance, easy-to-manage implementation that provides VM-to-datastore ratios that cannot be accomplished with other storage protocols such as Fibre Channel. This architecture can result in a 10x increase in datastore density with a correlating reduction in the number of datastores. With NFS the virtual infrastructure receives operational savings, because there are fewer storage pools to provision, manage, back up, replicate, and so on.

Through NFS, customers receive an integration of VMware virtualization technologies with WAFL®, NetApp's advanced data management and storage virtualization engine. This integration provides transparent access to VM-level storage virtualization offerings such as production-use data deduplication, immediate zero-cost VM and datastore clones, array-based thin provisioning, automated policy-based datastore resizing, and direct access to array-based Snapshot™ copies. NetApp provides integrated tools such as Site Recovery Manager, SnapManager for Virtual Infrastructure, the Rapid Cloning Utility, and the Virtual Storage Console.

2.6 SAN RAW DEVICE MAPPINGS

ESX allows for virtual machines to have direct access to LUNs for specific use cases such as P2V clustering or storage vendor management tools. This type of access is referred to as a raw device mapping (RDM) and can be configured with Fibre Channel, iSCSI, and Fibre Channel over Ethernet. In this design, ESX acts as a connection proxy between the VM and the storage array.

Unlike VMFS and NFS, RDMs are not used to provide shared datastores. Figure 4 shows an example of this configuration.

RDMs are an enabling technology for solutions such as virtual machine and physical-to-virtual-machine host-based clustering, such as with Microsoft® Cluster Server (MSCS). RDMs provide traditional LUN access to a host, so they can achieve high individual disk I/O performance, and they can be easily monitored for disk performance by a storage array.

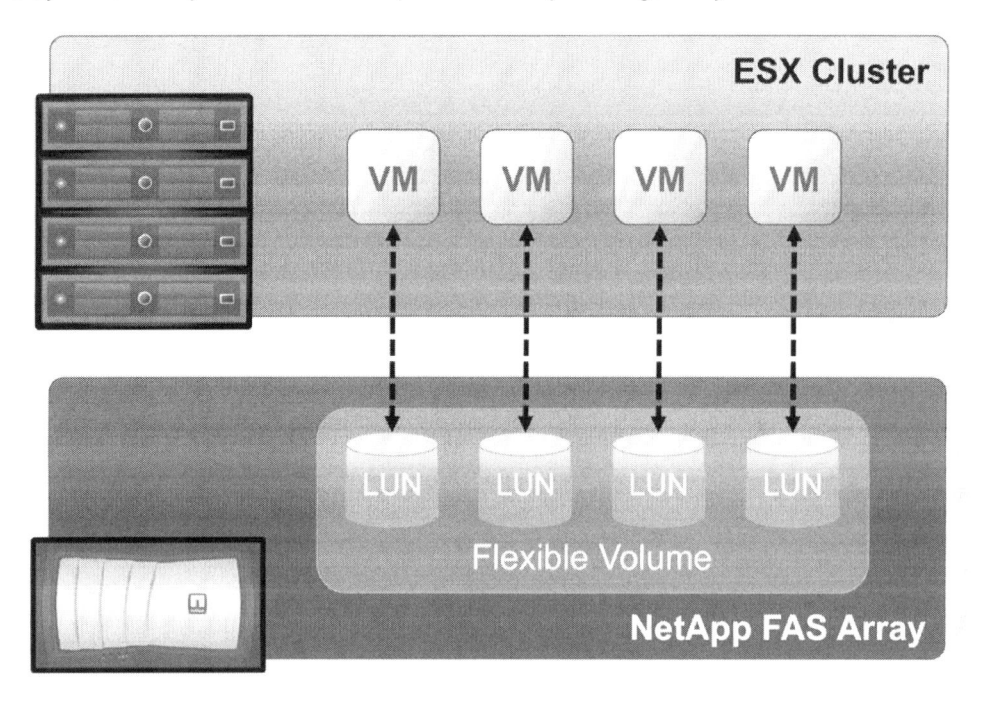

Figure 4) ESX cluster with VMs connected to RDM LUNs using FC or iSCSI.

RDM LUNS ON NETAPP

RDMs are available in two modes: physical and virtual. Both modes support key VMware features such as VMotion and can be used in both HA and DRS clusters. The key difference between the two technologies is the amount of SCSI virtualization that occurs at the VM level. This difference results in some limitations around MSCS and VMware snapshot use case scenarios.

NetApp enhances the use of RDMs by providing array-based LUN-level thin provisioning, production-use data deduplication, advanced integration components such as SnapDrive®, application specific Snapshot backups with the SnapManager for applications suite, and FlexClone® zero-cost cloning of RDM-based datasets.

Technical note: VMs running MSCS must use the path selection policy of MRU.

2.7 DATASTORE COMPARISON TABLES

Differentiating what is available with each type of datastore and storage protocol can require considering many points. The following table compares the features available with each storage option. A similar chart for VMware functionality is available in the VMware ESX and ESXi Server Configuration Guide.

Table 1) Datastore supported features.

Capability/Feature	FC/FCoE	iSCSI	NFS
Format	VMFS or RDM	VMFS or RDM	NetApp WAFL
Max number of datastores or LUNs	256	256	64
Max datastore size	64TB	64TB	16TB or 100TB*
Max LUN/NAS file system size	2TB minus 512 bytes	2TB minus 512 bytes	16TB or 100TB*
Optimal queue depth per LUN/file system	64	64	N/A
Available link speeds	4 and 8Gb FC and 10-Gigabit Ethernet (10GbE)	1 and 10GbE	1 and 10GbE

* 100TB requires 64-bit aggregates.

Table 2) VMware supported storage related functionality.

Capability/Feature	FC/FCoE	iSCSI	NFS
VMotion	Yes	Yes	Yes
Storage VMotion	Yes	Yes	Yes
VMware HA	Yes	Yes	Yes
DRS	Yes	Yes	Yes
VCB	Yes	Yes	Yes
MSCS within a VM	Yes, using RDM for shared LUNs	Initiator in GOS is supported by NetApp	Not supported
Fault Tolerance	Yes with eager-zeroed thick VMDKs, or virtual mode** RDMs	Yes with eager-zeroed thick VMDKs, or virtual mode** RDMs	Yes with eager-zeroed thick VMDKs
Site Recovery Manager	Yes	Yes	Yes
Thin-Provisioned VMs (virtual disks)	Yes	Yes	Yes*
VMware Native Multipathing	Yes	Yes	N/A
Boot from SAN	Yes	Yes with HBAs	No

* This is the default setting for all VMs on NetApp NFS
** NetApp SnapDrive for Windows® software does not support virtual-mode RDM devices.

Table 3) NetApp supported storage management features.

Capability/Feature	FC/FCoE	iSCSI	NFS
Data deduplication	Savings in the array	Savings in the array	Savings in the datastore
Thin provisioning	Datastore or RDM	Datastore or RDM	Datastore
Resize datastore	Grow only	Grow only	Grow, Autogrow, and Shrink
Thin provisioning	Datastore or RDM	Datastore or RDM	Datastore
SANscreen VM Insight	Yes	Yes	Yes
SnapDrive (in guest)	Yes	Yes	No*
ESX Host Utilities Virtual Storage Console (VSC 2.0)	Yes	Yes	Yes
VM Backup and Recovery using VSC 2.0	Yes	Yes	Yes
Provisioning and Cloning using VSC 2.0	Yes	Yes	Yes

* Support for NFS-managed VMDKs in SnapDrive is targeted for a future release of SnapDrive.

Table 4) Supported backup features.

Capability/Feature	FC/FCoE	iSCSI	NFS
Snapshot backups	Yes	Yes	Yes
Replicated backups support SRM	Yes	Yes	Yes
SnapMirror®	Datastore or RDM	Datastore or RDM	Datastore or VM
SnapVault®	Datastore or RDM	Datastore or RDM	Datastore or VM
VMDK image access	VCB	VCB	VCB, VIC File Explorer
VMDK file-level access	VCB, Windows only	VCB, Windows only	VCB and third-party apps
NDMP granularity	Datastore	Datastore	Datastore or VM

2.8 VMWARE VIRTUAL DISK FORMATS

There are three types of virtual disks available to VMs in vSphere. You should become familiar with each, including their similarities, differences, weaknesses, and strengths.

THE THICK VIRTUAL DISK

This is the traditional virtual disk format most of us have deployed with most of our VMs. This format preallocates the capacity of the virtual disk from the datastore at the time it is created. This format does not format the VMDK at the time of deployment. This means that data, which needs to be written, must pause while the blocks required to store the data are zeroed out. The operation occurs on demand at any time an area of the virtual disk, which has never been written to, is required to store data.

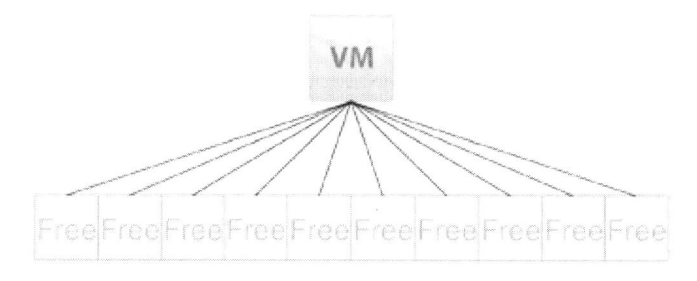

Thick VMDK
Blocks allocated in VMFS
Blocks not Allocated in Array
Blocks not formatted

Figure 5) A thick VMDK as it relates to storage blocks on an array.

THE THIN VIRTUAL DISK

This virtual disk form is very similar to the thick format, with the exception that it does not preallocate the capacity of the virtual disk from the datastore when it is created. When storage capacity is required, the VMDK allocates storage in chunks equal to the size of the file system block. For VMFS this is between 1MB and 8MB (size selected at deployment), and for NFS it is 4KB. The process of allocating blocks on a shared VMFS datastore is considered a metadata operation and as such executes SCSI locks on the datastore while the allocation operation is executed. While this process is very brief, it does suspend the write operations of the VMs on the datastore.

Thin VMDK
Blocks not allocated in VMFS
Blocks not allocated in Array
Blocks not formatted

Figure 6) A thin VMDK as it relates to storage blocks on an array.

Like the thick format, thin VMDKs are not formatted at the time of deployment. This also means that data that needs to be written must pause while the blocks required to store the data are zeroed out. The process of allocating blocks from within the datastore occurs on demand any time a write operation attempts to store data in a block range inside the VMDK that has not been written to by a previous operation.

To summarize the zeroing out and allocation differences between a thick and thin virtual disk, just remember that both suspend I/O when writing to new areas of disk that need to be zeroed, but before this can occur with a thin virtual disk, it might also have to obtain additional capacity from the datastore.

THE EAGER-ZEROED THICK VIRTUAL DISK

This virtual disk form is similar to the thick format as it preallocates the capacity of the virtual disk from the datastore when it is created; however, unlike the thick and thin formats an eager-zeroed thick virtual disk actually formats all of its data blocks at the time of deployment. This virtual disk format does not include or require the allocation and zeroing on-demand processes.

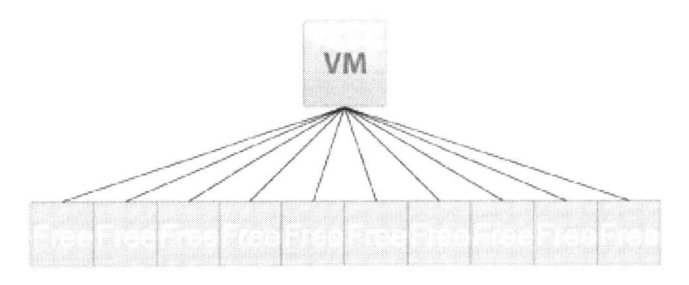

Figure 7) An eager-zeroed thick **VMDK** as it relates to storage blocks on an array.

2.9 INCREASING STORAGE USE

NetApp offers storage virtualization technologies that can enhance the storage savings provided by VMware thin-provisioning technology. FAS data deduplication and thin provisioning for VMFS datastores and RDM LUNs offer considerable storage savings by increasing storage use of the FAS array. Both of these technologies are native to NetApp arrays and do not require any configuration considerations or changes to be implemented within the ESX Servers.

By using the storage savings technologies of NetApp with VMware, you can increase server hardware use to match that of their physical servers. Reducing storage hardware results in reduced acquisition and operational costs.

Note: All virtual disks stored on NetApp NFS are thin-provisioned VMDKs and provide VMware clustering support.

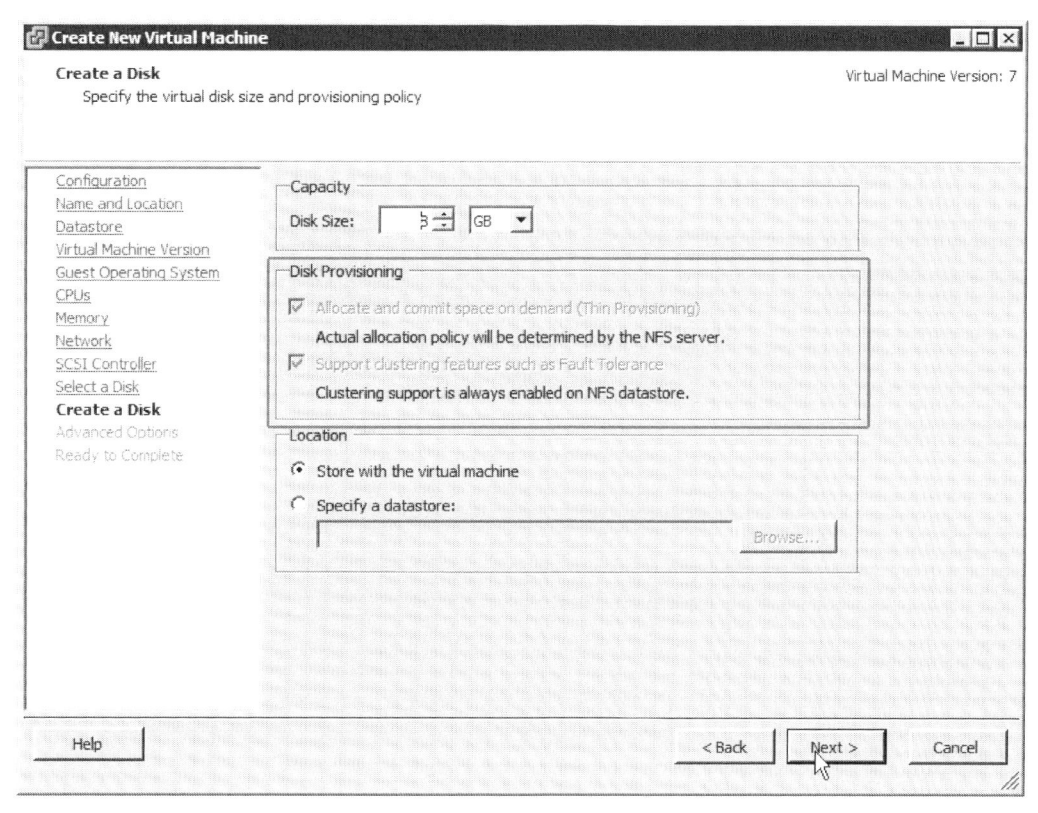

Figure 8) Note VMs deployed on NetApp NFS are always thin provisioned and provide clustering support.

2.10 STORAGE ARRAY THIN PROVISIONING

You should be very familiar with traditional storage provisioning and with the manner in which storage is preallocated and assigned to a server or in the case of VMware, a virtual machine. It is also a common practice for server administrators to overprovision storage in order to avoid running out of storage and the associated application downtime when expanding the provisioned storage. Although no system can be run at 100% storage use, there are methods of storage virtualization that allow administrators to address and oversubscribe storage in the same manner as with server resources (such as CPU, memory, networking, and so on). This form of storage virtualization is referred to as *thin provisioning*.

Traditional provisioning preallocates storage; thin provisioning provides storage on demand. The value of thin-provisioned storage is that storage is treated as a shared resource pool and is consumed only as each individual VM requires it. This sharing increases the total usage rate of storage by eliminating the unused but provisioned areas of storage that are associated with traditional storage. The drawback to thin provisioning and oversubscribing storage is that (without the addition of physical storage) if every VM requires its maximum possible storage at the same time, there will not be enough storage to satisfy the requests.

NetApp thin provisioning extends VMware thin provisioning for VMDKs and allows LUNs that are serving VMFS datastores to be provisioned to their total capacity yet consume only as much storage as is required to store the VMDK files (which can be of either thick or thin format). In addition, LUNs connected as RDMs can be thin provisioned.

NetApp recommends that when you enable NetApp thin-provisioned LUNs, you should deploy these LUNs in FlexVol® volumes that are also thin provisioned with a capacity that is 2x the size of the LUN. By deploying the LUN in this manner, the FlexVol volume acts merely as a quota. The storage consumed by the LUN is reported in FlexVol and its containing aggregate.

2.11 STORAGE ARRAY DATA DEDUPLICATION

One of the most popular VMware features is the ability to rapidly deploy new virtual machines from stored VM templates. A VM template includes a VM configuration file (.vmx) and one or more virtual disk files (.vmdk), which include an operating system, common applications, and patch files or system updates. Deploying from templates saves administrative time by copying the configuration and virtual disk files and registering this second copy as an independent VM. By design, this process introduces duplicate data for each new VM deployed. Figure 9 shows an example of typical storage consumption in a vSphere deployment.

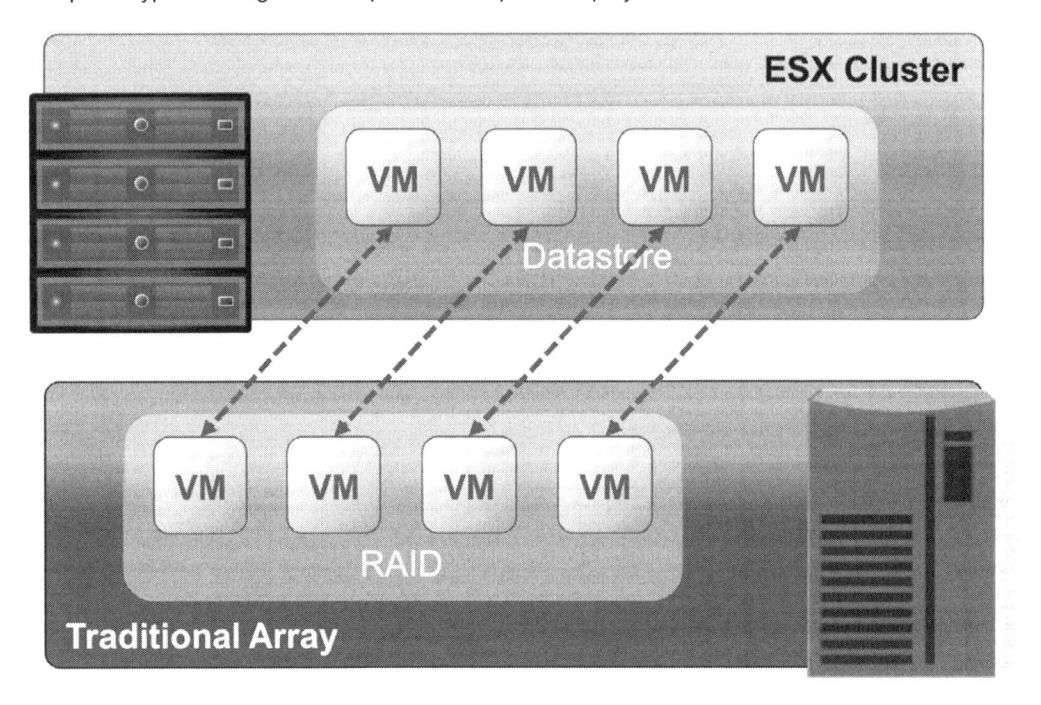

Figure 9) Storage consumption with a traditional array.

NetApp offers a data deduplication technology called *FAS data deduplication*. With NetApp FAS deduplication, VMware deployments can eliminate the duplicate data in their environment, enabling greater storage use. Deduplication virtualization technology enables multiple virtual machines to share the same physical blocks in a NetApp FAS system in the same manner that VMs share system memory. It can be seamlessly introduced into a virtual data center without having to make any changes to VMware administration, practices, or tasks. Deduplication runs on the NetApp FAS system at scheduled intervals and does not consume any CPU cycles on the ESX server. Figure 10 shows an example of the impact of deduplication on storage consumption in a vSphere deployment.

Deduplication is enabled on a volume, and the amount of data deduplication realized is based on the commonality of the data stored in a deduplication-enabled volume. For the largest storage savings, NetApp recommends grouping similar operating systems and similar applications into datastores, which ultimately reside on a deduplication-enabled volume.

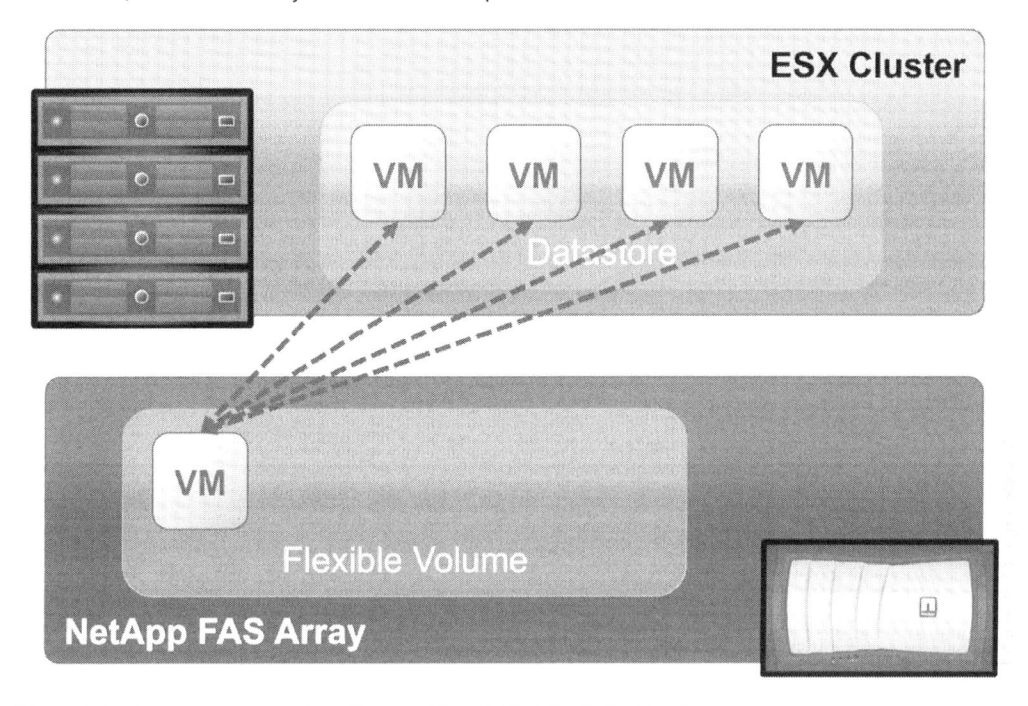

Figure 10) Storage consumption after enabling FAS data deduplication.

DEDUPLICATION CONSIDERATIONS WITH VMFS AND RDM LUNS

Enabling deduplication when provisioning LUNs produces storage savings. However, the default behavior of a LUN is to reserve an amount of storage equal to the provisioned LUN. This design means that although the storage array reduces the amount of capacity consumed, any gains made with deduplication are for the most part unrecognizable, because the space reserved for LUNs is not reduced.

To recognize the storage savings of deduplication with LUNs, you must enable NetApp LUN thin provisioning. Note that although deduplication reduces the amount of consumed storage, the VMware administrative team does not see this benefit directly, because its view of the storage is at a LUN layer, and LUNs always represent their provisioned capacity, whether they are traditional or thin provisioned. The NetApp Virtual Storage Console (VSC) provides the VI admin with the storage use at all layers in the storage stack.

NetApp recommends that when you enable dedupe on thin-provisioned LUNs, you should deploy these LUNs in FlexVol volumes that are also thin provisioned with a capacity that is 2x the size of the LUN. By deploying the LUN in this manner, the FlexVol volume acts merely as a quota. The storage consumed by the LUN is reported in FlexVol and its containing aggregate.

DEDUPLICATION ADVANTAGES WITH NFS

Unlike with LUNs, when deduplication is enabled with NFS, the storage savings are immediately available and recognized by the VMware administrative team. The benefit of dedupe is transparent to storage and VI admin teams. No special considerations are required for its usage.

DEDUPLICATION MANAGEMENT WITH VMWARE

Through the NetApp vCenter plug-ins, VMware administrators have the ability to enable, disable, and update data deduplication on a datastore-by-datastore basis. The details on this capability are covered in section 5, "vSphere Dynamic Storage Provisioning and Management."

2.12 VSTORAGE ARRAY INTEGRATION IN VMWARE VSPHERE 4.1

With the release of vSphere 4.1 VMware has delivered a set of storage constructs enhancing storage array integration in vSphere. These enhancements consist of three main components: vStorage APIs for array integration (VAAI), storage I/O control (SIOC), and storage performance statistics.

VSTORAGE APIS FOR ARRAY INTEGRATION (VAAI)

VAAI provides a mechanism for the acceleration of certain functions typically performed at the hypervisor by offloading these operations to the storage array. The goal of VAAI is to enable greater scalability at the host layer by freeing hypervisor resources (CPU, memory, I/O, and so on) during operations such as provisioning and cloning. This first release of VAAI provides support for new features only in VMFS datastores. In the case of NFS datastores on NetApp storage, many operations with respect to VM provisioning and cloning are already offloaded to the storage array with the combined capabilities of the Virtual Storage Console and file-level FlexClone. The initial release of VAAI expands VMFS to include similar capabilities. Within the current release of VAAI there are three capabilities:

- **Full copy**: When a data copy is initiated from the ESX/ESXi host, VAAI enables the storage array to perform that copy within the array, without the host having to read and write the data. This reduces the time and network load of cloning and migrating VMs with vMotion.
- **Block zeroing**: When a new virtual disk is created, such as an eager-zeroed thick VMDK, the disk must be formatted and written full of zeroes. VAAI allows the storage array to format zeroes into the disks, removing this workload from the host.
- **Hardware-assisted locking**: VMFS is a shared cluster file system and therefore requires management of metadata and locking to make sure that multiple hosts do not gain write access to the same data simultaneously. VAAI provides an alternative method of locking to that of SCSI-2 reservations used in previous releases. This new method of locking is managed automatically by the host and storage array and allows for greater scalability of VMFS datastores.

VAAI support requires that the storage array is running an operating system version that provides support. To use VAAI the NetApp array must be running NetApp Data ONTAP version 8.0.1, which is due to be released late in 2010. VAAI is enabled by default in Data ONTAP and in ESX/ESXi. Version 2.0 of the Virtual Storage Console indicates whether or not a storage array supports VAAI and if VAAI is enabled on that array.

STORAGE I/O CONTROL (SIOC)

The Storage I/O Control feature introduced in vSphere 4.1 enables quality of service control for storage using the concepts of shares and limits in the same way CPU and memory resources have been managed in the past. SIOC allows the administrator to make sure that certain VMs are given priority access to storage compared to other VMs, based on the allocation of resource shares, maximum IOPS limits, and whether or not the datastore has reached a specified congestion threshold. SIOC is currently only supported on FC or iSCSI VMFS datastores.

To use SIOC it must be enabled on the datastore and then resource shares and limits applied to the VMs in that datastore. The VM limits are applied on the Resources tab in the VM Edit Settings dialog window. By default all VMs in the datastore are given equal resource shares and unlimited IOPS.

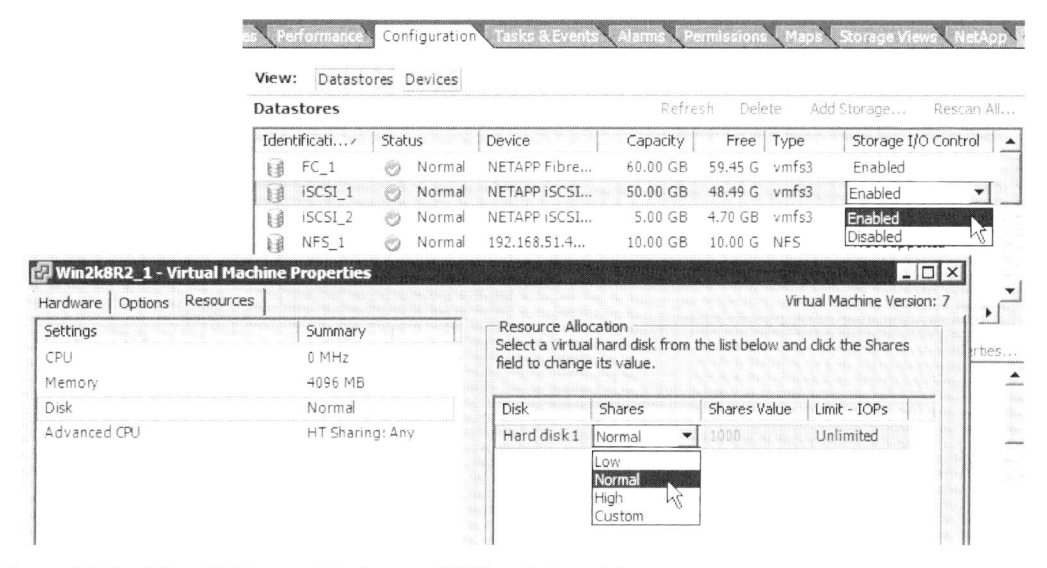

Figure 11) Enabling SIOC on a datastore and VM in vSphere 4.0.

Keep in mind that SIOC does not take action to limit storage throughput of a VM based on the value of its resource shares until the datastore congestion threshold is met. As long as the overall performance of the datastore is sufficient, according to the threshold, all VMs on the datastore have equal access to the storage. The congestion threshold is set per datastore in a value of milliseconds of latency. The default value is 30ms, and most environments do not need to adjust this value. Storage resource shares are set in values of low, normal, and high; these values are 500, 1000, and 2000, respectively, or a custom value might be set.

The amount of resource shares is used to determine how much throughput one VM is given as compared to another VM on the same datastore where SIOC is enabled. For example, when SIOC limitations are imposed on the datastore, a VM with 1,000 shares is entitled to twice the access to resources as a VM with 500 shares. The actual amount of throughput achievable by each VM is dependent on the demands of the VMs. Viewing the shares settings of multiple VMs can be done in the vSphere client datastores view by selecting a datastore, then the virtual machine tab.

A VM's access to a datastore can also be limited to a maximum storage IOPS. Setting a maximum IOPS limit on a VM causes vSphere to continuously limit that VM's throughput to that number of IOPS, even if the congestion threshold has not been surpassed. To limit a VM to a certain amount of throughput in MB/sec, you must use the IOPS limit by setting an appropriate maximum IOPS value according to the VM's typical I/O size: for example, to limit a VM with a typical I/O size of 8k to 10MB/sec of throughput, set the maximum IOPS for the VM to 1,280. The following formula might be used: MB/sec ÷ I/O size = IOPS. Example: 10,240,000 ÷ 8,000 = 1,280.

STORAGE PERFORMANCE STATISTICS

An additional storage enhancement in vSphere 4.1 is an increase in available storage performance statistics available both in vCenter and the esxtop command. In VI3 environments gathering storage performance metrics directly in vCenter was limited to viewing performance of specific physical disks. This allowed for some ability to monitor storage performance per datastore on NetApp storage arrays because a typical FC datastore in a NetApp environment is made up of one LUN presented from the storage system and would be represented as one physical disk in the vCenter performance monitor. Where multiple disks or LUNs were used to make up one datastore, it was difficult to isolate complete datastore performance; this limitation continued into vSphere 4.0. Additionally, the ability to view metrics per NFS datastore or individual virtual disks attached to VMs was not available in both VI3 and vSphere 4.0. The metrics viewable for hosts and VMs in vSphere 4.0 are shown in Figure 12.

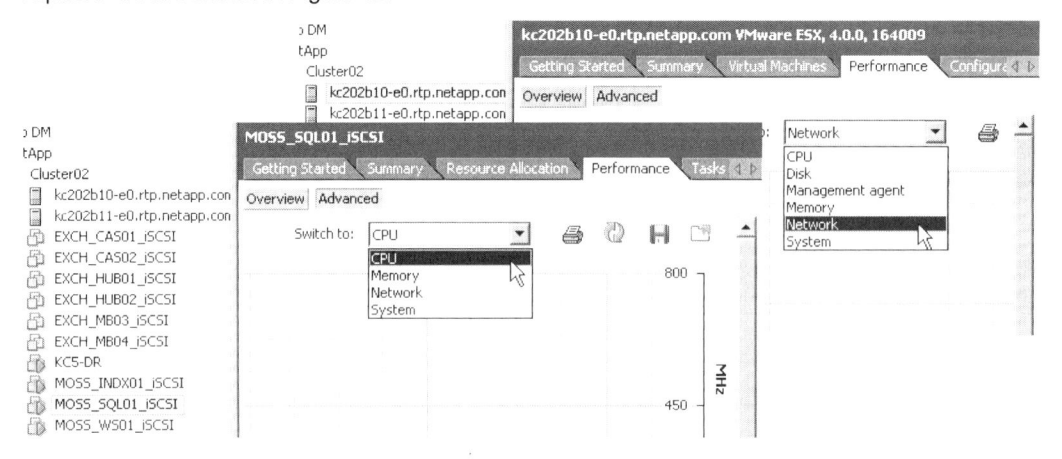

Figure 12) Performance statistics available in vSphere 4.0.

The additional performance statics available in vSphere 4.1 allow the virtual administrator to view host I/O statistics per datastore storage path and per storage adapter in FC environments. Datastore performance reporting is available with all storage protocols: FC, iSCSI, and NFS. VM performance metrics now include datastore performance per VM and performance per virtual disk. Figure 13 shows the additional performance metrics available in vSphere 4.1.

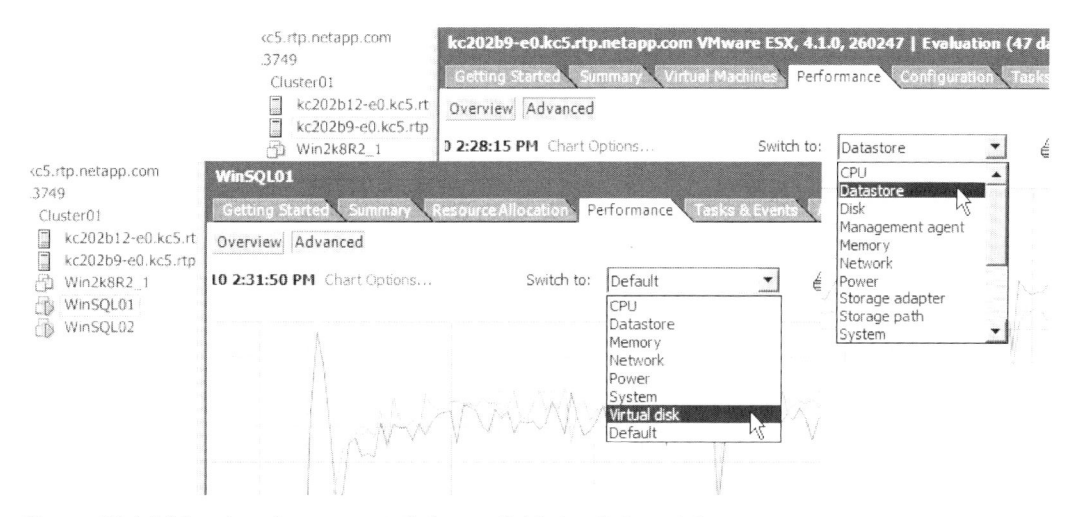

Figure 13) Additional performance statistics available in vSphere 4.1.

A particular challenge in NAS environments has been the inability to determine which NFS datastores are most active or which virtual disks of a VM are most active. Figure 14 is an example of the per virtual disk metrics in vSphere 4.1.

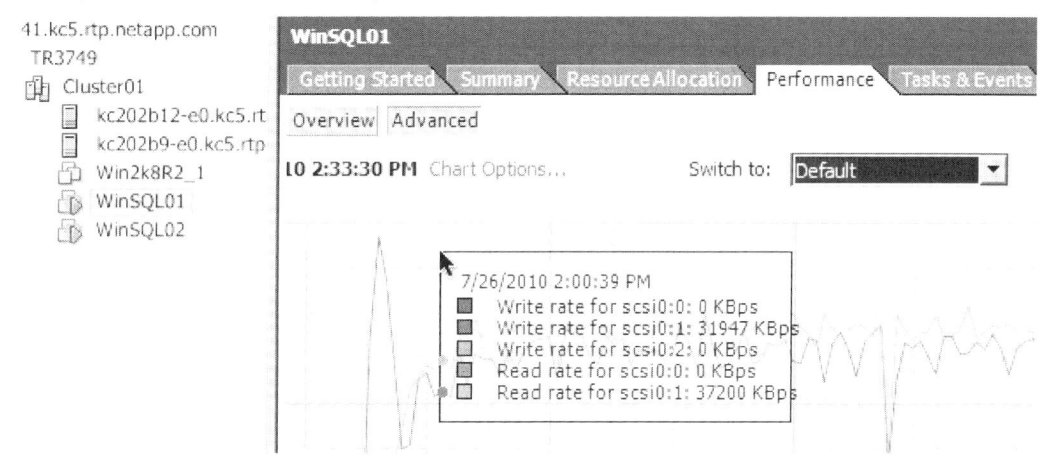

Figure 14) Per virtual disk performance statistics available in vSphere 4.1.

Table 5) Storage performance statistics capabilities by protocol and vSphere version.

Object	Component	Statistic	Storage Protocol	Available in	
				vCenter	ESXTOP*
ESX/ESXi Host	Datastore	Throughput and latency	FC, iSCSI, NFS	4.1	4.1
	Storage Adapter	Throughput and latency	FC	4.1	4.0+
	Storage Path	Throughput and latency	FC	4.1	4.0+

Object	Component	Statistic	Storage Protocol	Available in	
				vCenter	ESXTOP*
	LUN	Throughput and latency	FC, iSCSI	4.0+	4.0+
Virtual Machine	Datastore	Throughput and latency	FC, iSCSI, NFS	4.1	4.1
	Virtual Disk	Throughput and latency	FC, iSCSI, NFS	4.1	4.1

* Access to esxtop for ESXi hosts requires the use of the vSphere CLI resxtop command.

3 STORAGE NETWORK DESIGN AND SETUP

This section applies to:

NetApp Go further, faster	**Storage Administrators**
vmware	**VI Administrators**
CISCO	**Network Administrators**

The goal of any storage network is to provide uninterrupted service to all nodes connecting to it. In this section we focus primarily on how to establish a highly available Ethernet storage network. The reasons for focusing on Ethernet are twofold. First, Fibre Channel storage networks provide a single service, Fibre Channel. As such, these single-purpose networks are simpler to design and deploy in a highly available configuration. Second, the current industry trend is solely focused on multipurposed Ethernet networks (converged networks) that provide storage, voice, and user access.

PRODUCTION STORAGE NETWORKS

Regardless of protocol, a storage network must address the following three goals:

- Be redundant across switches in a multiswitch environment
- Use as many available physical paths as possible
- Be scalable across multiple physical interfaces or ports

3.1 SAN AND NAS STORAGE NETWORKING BASICS

With vSphere the primary difference between SAN and NAS storage networking is in the area of multipathing. In the current versions of ESX/ESXi, NFS requires manual static path configuration whereas iSCSI, FC, and FCoE are available with both manual and automated multipathing options (note that iSCSI requires additional configuration options prior to implementing).

Multipathing and datastore security in the form of NFS exports and (iSCSI FC, and FCoE) LUN masking is dynamically assigned when the VMware administrative team provisions storage. The details of this automation are covered with the RCU in section 5, "vSphere Dynamic Storage Provisioning and Management."

3.2 FIBRE CHANNEL STORAGE NETWORKING BASICS

Fibre Channel storage networks makes up a large percentage of mature VMware storage infrastructures. This market share is attributed to FC being the first networked-attached storage protocol supported by ESX in version 2.0. While FC is a well-known and mature technology, this section covers best practices for deploying VMware on Fibre Channel with NetApp storage arrays.

CONNECTIVITY BASICS

ESX servers and NetApp storage arrays connect to a SAN fabric using host bus adapters (HBAs). Connectivity to FCoE fabrics is enabled through converged network adapters (CNAs). Each HBA/CNA can run as either an initiator (ESX/ESXi) or as a target (NetApp). Each adapter has a global unique address referred to as a World Wide Name (WWN). Each WWN is required to be known in order to configure LUN access on a NetApp storage array.

Both NetApp and VMware highly recommend that as a best practice each ESX/ESXi host should have at least two adapter ports. For more information on VMware FC best practices and recommendations, see THE "VMware Fibre Channel SAN Configuration Guide."

FABRIC ZONING RECOMMENDATION

Many devices and nodes can be attached to a SAN, and a way to secure access and optimize I/O access to these devices is by implementing zones. SAN zoning is a method of arranging Fibre Channel devices into logical groups over the physical configuration of the fabric or Fibre Channel network.

Zoning is available in hardware (hard zoning) or in software (soft zoning). An option available with both implementations is port zoning, where physical ports define security zones. A host's access to a LUN is determined by what physical port it connects to. With port zoning, zone information must be updated every time a user changes switch ports. In addition, port zoning does not allow zones to overlap.

Another form of zoning is WWN zoning, where the fabric leverages its name servers to either allow or block access to particular World Wide Port Names (WWPNs) in the fabric. A major advantage of WWPN zoning is the ability to recable the fabric without having to modify the zone members.

NetApp and VMware highly recommend that customers implement "single-initiator, multiple storage target" zones. This design offers an ideal balance of simplicity and availability with FC and FCoE deployments. For assistance, in identifying the WWN or IQN of the ESX server, select Storage Adapters on the Configuration tab for each ESX/ESXi host in vCenter Server and refer to the WWN Identifier column.

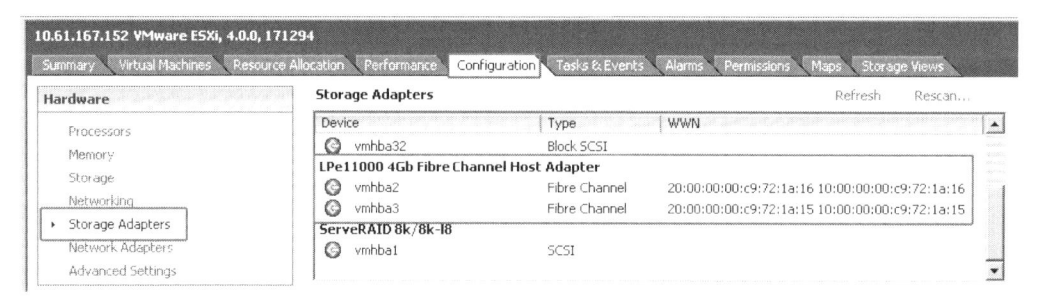

Figure 15) Identifying WWPN and IQN numbers in the vCenter client.

3.3   ETHERNET STORAGE NETWORKING BASICS

10GBE OR DATA CENTER ETHERNET

NetApp Data ONTAP and VMware ESX/ESXi 4 both provide support for 10GbE. An advantage of 10GbE is the ability to reduce the number of network ports in the infrastructure, especially but not limited to blade servers. To verify support for your hardware and its use for storage I/O, see the ESX I/O compatibility guide.

VLAN TAGGING OR 802.1Q

When segmenting network traffic with VLANs, interfaces either can be dedicated to a single VLAN or can support multiple VLANs with VLAN tagging.

For systems that have fewer NICs, such as blade servers, VLANs can be very useful. Channeling two NICs together provides an ESX server with physical link redundancy. By adding multiple VLANs, you can group common IP traffic onto separate VLANs for optimal performance. It is recommended that service console access with the virtual machine network should be on one VLAN, and the VMkernel activities of IP storage and VMotion should be on a second VLAN.

VLANs and VLAN tagging also play a simple but important role in securing an IP storage network. NFS exports can be restricted to a range of IP addresses that are available only on the IP storage VLAN. NetApp storage appliances also allow the restriction of the iSCSI protocol to specific interfaces and/or VLAN tags. These simple configuration settings have an enormous effect on the security and availability of IP-based datastores. If you are using multiple VLANs over the same interface, make sure that sufficient throughput can be provided for all traffic.

FLOW CONTROL

Flow control is the process of managing the rate of data transmission between two nodes to prevent a fast sender from overrunning a slow receiver. Flow control can be configured on ESX/ESXi servers, FAS storage arrays, and network switches. It is recommended to configure the endpoints, ESX servers, and NetApp arrays with flow control set to "send on" and "receive off."

After these settings have been configured on the storage controller and network switch ports, it results in the desired configuration without modifying the flow control settings in ESX/ESXi. For details on setting flow control in vSphere, see VMware KB 1013413.

For network switches it is recommended to set the switch ports connecting to ESX hosts and FAS storage arrays to either "Desired" or, if this mode is not available, set these ports to "send off" and "receive on."

Note: The switch ports are configured with settings opposite to those of the ESX/ESXi and FAS systems.

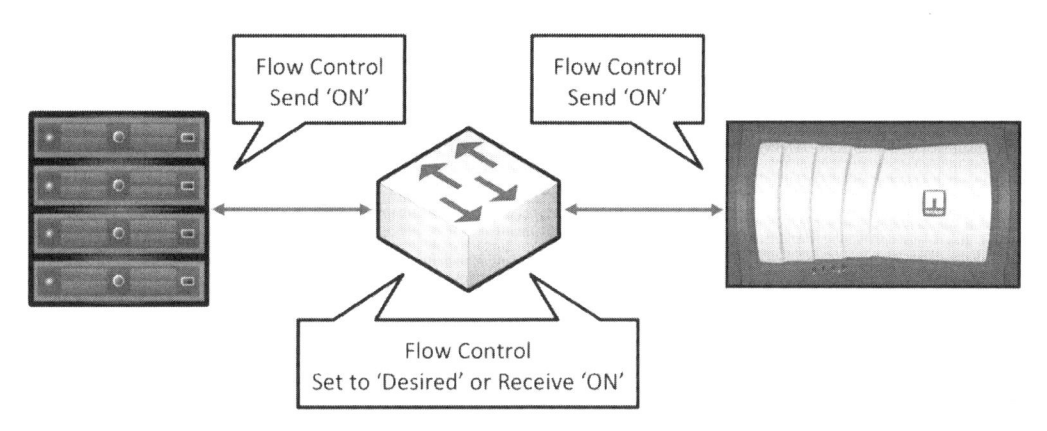

Figure 16) Configuring flow control settings.

SPANNING TREE PROTOCOL

Spanning Tree Protocol (STP) is a network protocol that makes sure of a loop-free topology for any bridged LAN. In the OSI model for computer networking, STP falls under the OSI Layer-2. STP allows a network design to include spare (redundant) links to provide automatic backup paths if an active link fails, without the danger of bridge loops, or the need for manual enabling/disabling of these backup links. Bridge loops must be avoided because they result in flooding the network.

When connecting ESX and NetApp storage arrays to Ethernet storage networks, it is highly recommended that the Ethernet ports to which these systems connect be configured as either RSTP edge ports or using the Cisco feature portfast. If your environment is using the Cisco portfast feature and you have 802.1q VLAN trunking enabled to either ESX server or NetApp storage arrays, it is suggested that you enable the spanning-tree portfast trunk feature.

When a port is configured as an edge port on an RSTP-enabled switch, the edge port immediately transitions its forwarding state to active. This immediate transition was previously recognized as a Cisco proprietary feature named portfast. Ports that connect to other switch ports should not be configured with the edge port or portfast feature.

ROUTING AND IP STORAGE NETWORKS

Whenever possible, NetApp recommends that you configure storage networks as a single network that does not route. This model helps to make sure of performance and provides a layer of data security.

ENABLING JUMBO FRAMES

When enabling jumbo frames throughout an infrastructure, there are two classifications of devices. Those classifications are devices that transmit jumbo frames (NetApp storage, ESX server) and devices that transport jumbo frames (Ethernet switches). Devices that transmit jumbo frames are sometimes configured to use VLAN trunking, while other devices are not. An Ethernet frame consists of a payload, Ethernet header (18 bytes), and sometimes a VLAN tag (4 bytes, if enabled). Devices that transmit jumbo frames generally have a user administratively define the payload size. The system then appends the Ethernet header and VLAN tag, causing the frame, which is transmitted from the device, to range from 9,018 bytes or 9,022 bytes (with VLAN tagging). It is because of this frame size variation that it is a best practice to set the devices that transport jumbo frames (Ethernet switches) to their maximum allowable setting.

In today's modern data center class switches, that maximum is typically 9,216 bytes. If the switching infrastructure being used does not accommodate this size, you must make sure of the endpoint frame size you configure and append the Ethernet header and VLAN tag. If your infrastructure is not configured to accommodate the payload plus header and VLAN tag, your environment either will not successfully negotiate communications or will suffer severe performance penalties.

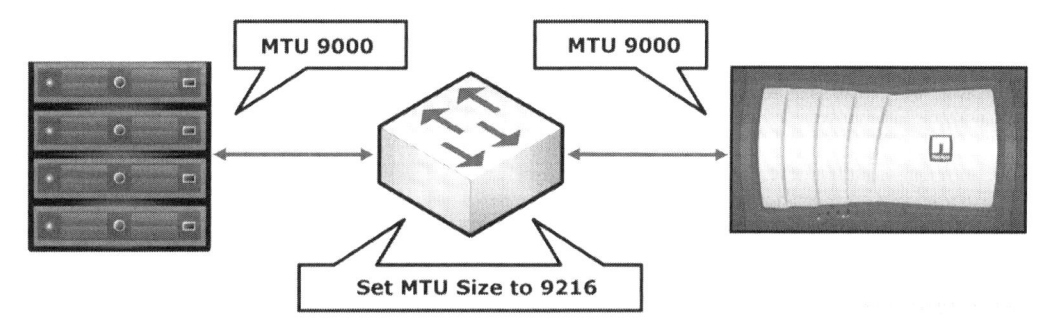

Figure 17) An overview of the MTU size required with jumbo frames.

ESX/ESXi hosts require creating a vSwitch that supports jumbo frames followed by a VMkernel port, which is assigned to the vSwitch.

To enable jumbo frames on a vSwitch, follow these steps:

1. Connect to an ESX/ESXi host (using vSphere CLI).
2. To configure, execute the following command:

```
vicfg-vswitch -m <MTU> <vSwitch>
```

This command sets the MTU for all uplinks on that vSwitch. Set the MTU size to the largest MTU size among all the virtual network adapters connected to the vSwitch.

3. To verify the configuration, execute the following command:

```
vicfg-vswitch -l
```

To enable jumbo frames on a VMkernel port, follow these steps.

1. Connect to an ESX/ESXi host (using vSphere CLI).
2. To configure, execute the following command:

```
esxcfg-vmknic -a -I <ip address> -n <netmask> -m <MTU> <port group
name>
```

This command creates a VMkernel port with jumbo frame support.

3. To verify the configuration, execute the following command:

```
esxcfg-vmknic -l
```

To set the MTU size on a FAS array, open NSM, select the network configuration for the array and the interface, and edit. See Figure 18. Repeat for each array and interface requiring jumbo frames.

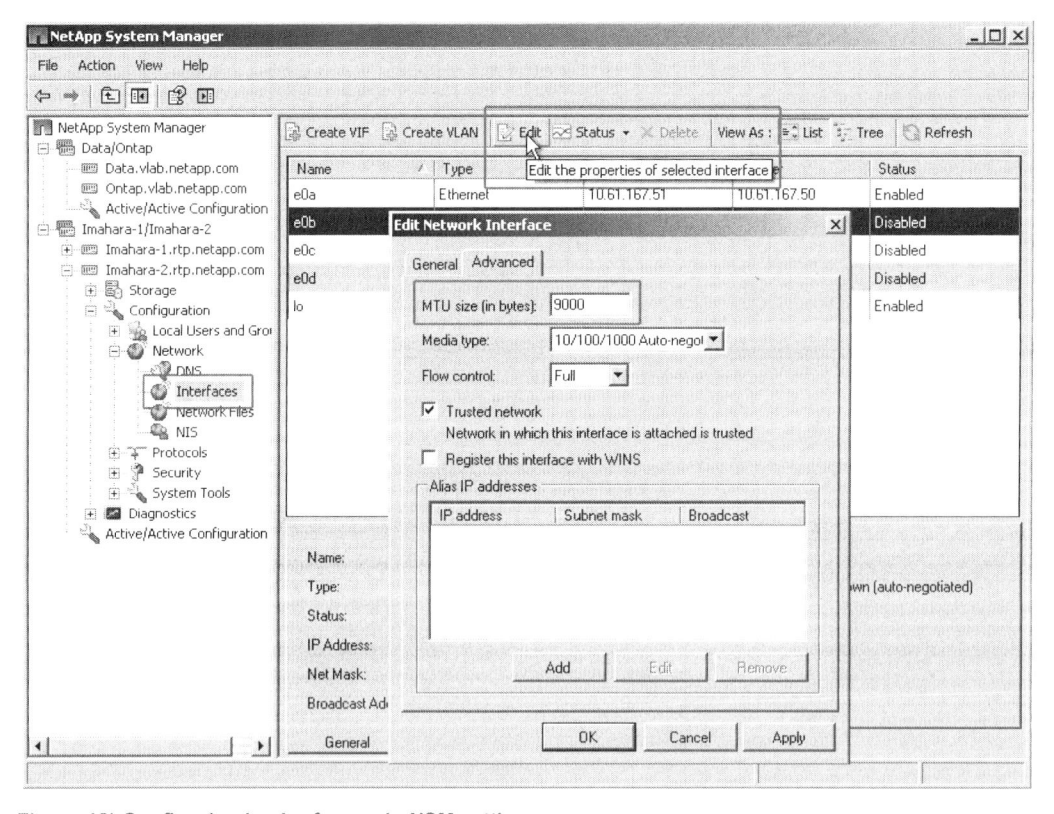

Figure 18) Configuring jumbo frames in NSM settings.

SEPARATE ETHERNET STORAGE NETWORK

As a best practice NetApp recommends separating IP-based storage traffic from public IP network traffic by implementing separate physical network segments or VLAN segments. This design follows the architecture of SCSI and FC connectivity.

Creating a second network in ESX requires creating a second vSwitch to separate the traffic onto other physical NICs. The ESX server requires a VMkernel port to be defined on the new vSwitch.

VMware best practices with HA clusters recommend each ESX server has a second service console port defined. When using IP-based storage networking, this is a convenient network, which you can use to add this second SC port.

With this design, NetApp recommends not allowing routing of data between the storage or VMkernel and other networks. In other words, do not define a default gateway for the VMkernel storage network. With this model, NFS deployments require a second service console port be defined on the VMkernel storage virtual switch within each ESX server.

IP storage network, or VMkernel, connectivity can be verified by the use of the vmkping command. With NFS connected datastores, the syntax to test connectivity is `vmkping <NFS IP address>`.

NETAPP VIRTUAL INTERFACES (AKA ETHERCHANNEL)

A virtual network interface (VIF) or EtherChannel is a mechanism that supports aggregation of network interfaces into one logical interface unit. Once created, a VIF is indistinguishable from a physical network interface. VIFs are used to provide fault tolerance of the network connection and in some cases higher throughput to the storage device.

NetApp enables the use of two types of load-balancing VIFs: manual multimode and dynamic LACP (IEEE 802.3ad). NetApp also provides an active-passive form of VIF, referred to as a single-mode VIF. NetApp VIFs might also be grouped and layered into a form of second-level VIF, referred to in this document as layered multimode EtherChannel.

Multimode VIFs are static configured EtherChannels. In a multimode VIF, all of the physical connections in the VIF are simultaneously active and can carry traffic. This mode requires that all of the interfaces be connected to a switch that supports trunking or aggregation over multiple port connections. The switch must be configured to understand that all the port connections share a common MAC address and are part of a single logical interface. In the event of a physical interface failure resulting in the loss of link, the VIF automatically transmits traffic on the surviving links in the VIF without loss of connectivity.

LACP VIFs are dynamic (IEEE 802.3ad) compliant EtherChannels. In an LACP VIF, all of the physical connections are simultaneously active and carry traffic as with multimode VIFs, described earlier. LACP VIFs introduce signaling transmissions between the storage controller and the network switch. This signaling informs the remote channeling partner of link status, and if a failure or inability to transmit data on a link is observed, the device identifying this problem informs the remote channeling partner of the failure, causing the removal of the interface from the EtherChannel. This feature differs from standard multimode VIFs in that there is no signaling between channel partners to inform the remote partner of link failure. The only means for an interface to be removed from a standard multimode VIF is loss of link.

Multimode and LACP EtherChannels both use the same algorithms for determining IP load balancing. These algorithms are based on source and destination IP, MAC address, or TCP/UDP port number. NetApp recommends using IP-based source and destination load balancing, especially when the network is designed to route storage traffic as it provides load-balancing capabilities, which works in the broadest set of storage network configurations.

In a single-mode VIF, only one of the physical connections is active at a time. If the storage controller detects a fault in the active connection, a standby connection is activated. No configuration is necessary on the switch to use a single-mode VIF, and the physical interfaces that make up the VIF do not have to connect to the same switch. Note that IP load balancing is not supported on single-mode VIFs.

3.4   CISCO NEXUS 1000V VNETWORK DISTRIBUTED SWITCH RECOMMENDATIONS

CISCO NEXUS 1000V SYSTEM VLAN

When deploying the 1000V vNetwork Distributed Switch (vDS), be aware that it is composed of two components, the Virtual Supervisor Module (VSM) and the Virtual Ethernet Module (VEM).

The VSM runs as a virtual machine and is the brains of the operation with a 1000V. Should the VSM fail, traffic continues; however, management of the vDS is suspended. VSMs should be deployed in an active-passive pair. These two VSAs should never reside on the same physical ESX server. This configuration can be controlled by DRS policies.

The VEM is embedded in all ESX/ESXi hosts, and it is managed by the VSM. One exists for each host in the cluster that is participating in the Cisco Nexus 1000V vDS.

There is a possibility that should a VSM be managing the links to the datastore that stores the VSM VM, the VSM failover process might not occur. In order to avoid this scenario, it is the recommendation of NetApp and Cisco to make sure that all service console and VMkernel interfaces (vswif and vmknic) reside on a system VLAN. System VLANs are defined by an optional parameter that can be added in a port profile. Do not configure a VM network as a system VLAN.

ENABLING JUMBO FRAMES

While the Cisco Nexus 1000V vDS supports the use of jumbo frames, it lacks the ability to create or enable jumbo frames on VMkernel interfaces. In order to use jumbo frames with VMkernel ports, you must first create a traditional vSwitch and VMkernel port, enable support for jumbo frames, and import these ports into a 1000V vDS. To enable jumbo frames on a vSwitch, follow these steps.

1. Configure a vSwitch and VMkernel ports for jumbo frame support (section 3.3).
2. Connect to ESX/ESXi host using vCenter client.
3. Assign the VMkernel port created above to the vSwitch created earlier.
4. Migrate the vSwitch to a 1000V vDS (see Figure 19).

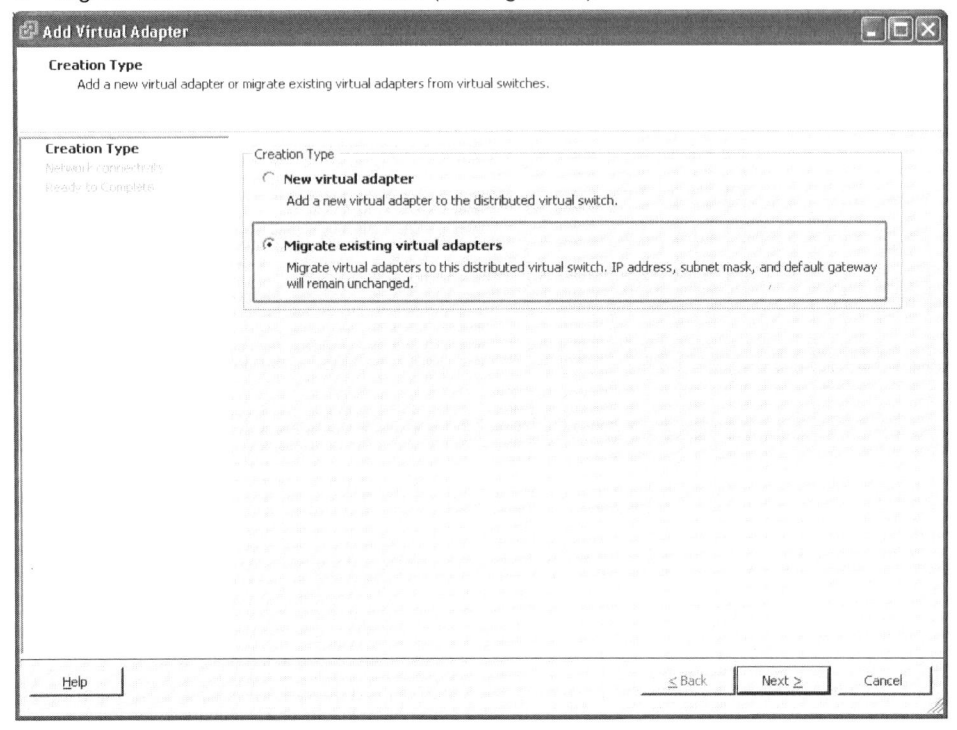

Figure 19) Migrating a virtual adapter from a vSwitch to a 1000V.

3.5 SWITCHING CAPABILITIES DETERMINE THE STORAGE NETWORK ARCHITECTURE

The storage design you implement is dictated based on the capabilities of your network switches. The ideal configuration is to have Ethernet switches that support multiswitch link aggregation (MSLA). If you have a switch with this capability such as Cisco Nexus (virtual port channels), Cisco Catalyst 3750 series (cross-stack EtherChannel), or Cisco Catalyst 6500 series with VSS 1440 modules (multichassis EtherChannel), the design and architecture required for your network will be rather simple.

Proceed to section 3.6 to configure this type of switching technology.

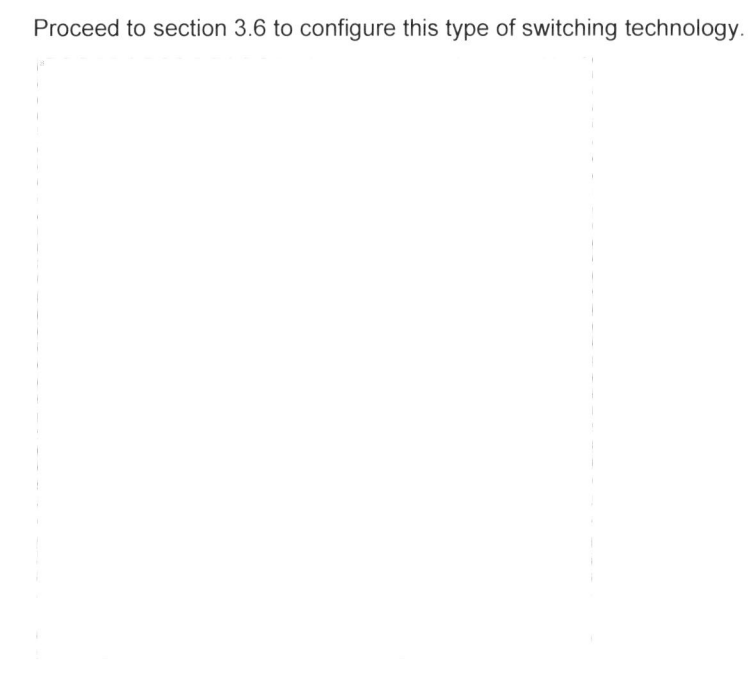

Figure 20) An overview of multiswitch link aggregation.

Alternatively, if your network operates with more traditional switching technology, one that lacks multiswitch link aggregation, you are required to complete some additional configuration steps in ESX/ESXi, Data ONTAP, and the switch configuration.

Figure 21) An overview of traditional switches.

Proceed to section 3.7 to configure this type of switching technology.

3.6 STORAGE NETWORK ARCHITECTURE WITH MULTISWITCH LINK AGGREGATION

In this configuration, the IP switches to be used for the Ethernet storage network support multiswitch link aggregation. As such, each storage controller requires one physical connection to each switch; the two ports connected to each storage controller are then combined into one multimode LACP VIF with IP load balancing enabled. This design provides multiple active links to each storage controller, provides a means to scale throughput by simply adding more links, and requires multiple IP addresses per controller, and each uses two physical links for each active network connection in order to achieve path high availability.

ADVANTAGES OF MSLA

- Provides multiple active connections to each storage controller.
- Easily scales to more connections by adding NICs and aliases.
- Storage controller connection load balancing is automatically managed by the EtherChannel IP load-balancing policy.

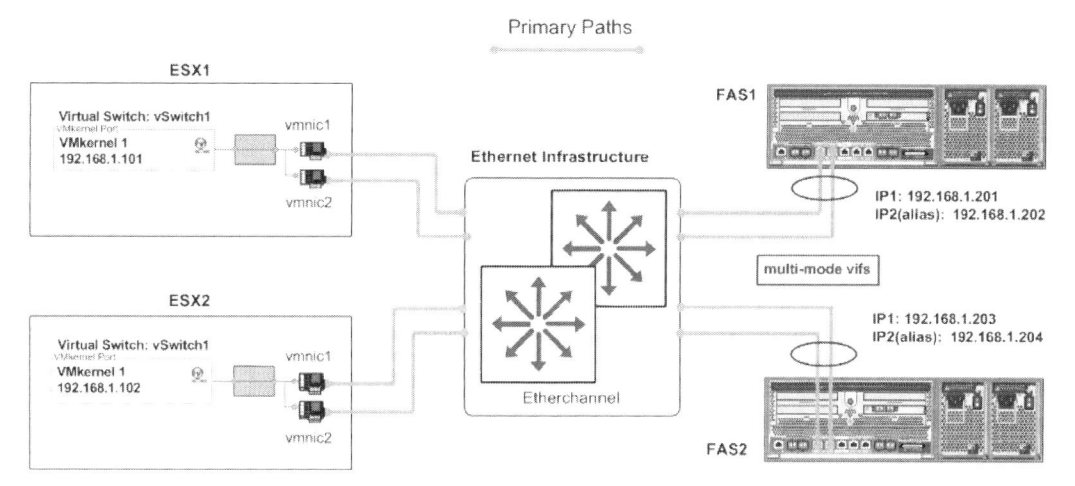

Figure 22) Storage side multimode VIFs using multiswitch EtherChannel.

STORAGE LOAD BALANCING

Using multiple physical paths simultaneously on an IP storage network requires EtherChannel ports and multiple IP addresses on the storage controller. This model results in a design that balances datastore connectivity across all interfaces. This balancing is handled by the RCU at the time the datastore is provisioned.

Figure 23 shows an overview of storage traffic flow when using multiple ESX servers and multiple datastores.

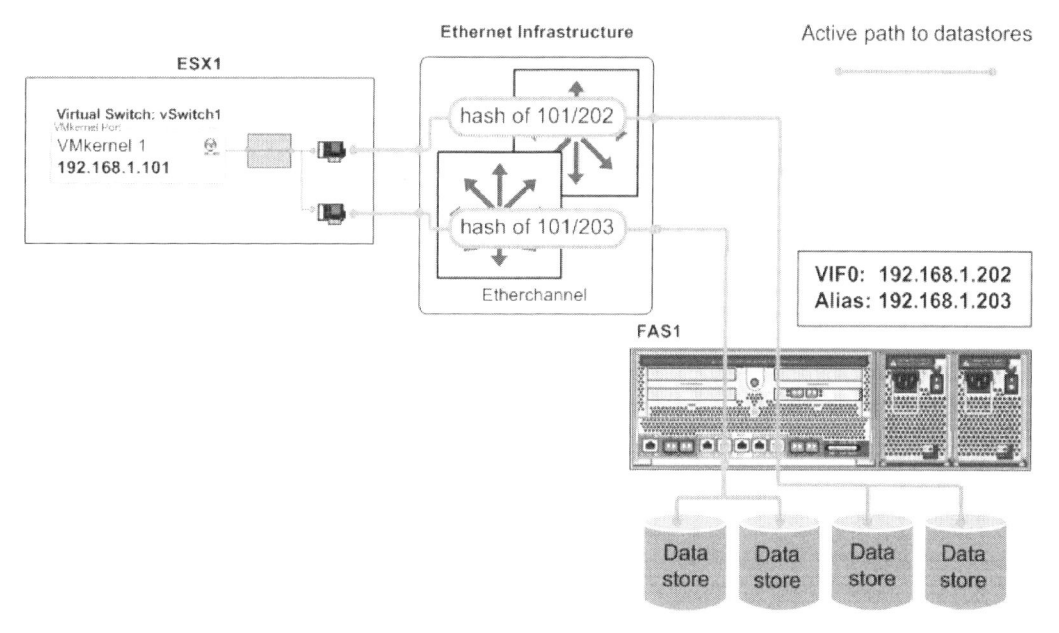

Figure 23) Datastore connections with multiswitch EtherChannel.

CONFIGURING NETAPP STORAGE NETWORK PORTS

If your plans are to deploy with IP-based storage access, NFS, or iSCSI, then you need to configure multiple Ethernet links to operate together as an EtherChannel. EtherChannel provides aggregated bandwidth and link availability from the network switches to the storage controller. This design is recommended, because the storage controller handles the aggregated I/O load from all ESX/ESXI nodes.

NetApp supports all modes of EtherChannels that are compliant with 802.3ad LACP and/or static EtherChannels. In Data ONTAP EtherChannels are referred to as virtual interfaces (VIFs). NetApp recommends that you configure your EtherChannel or VIFs as LACP whenever possible.

For use in a multiswitch link aggregation configuration, you need to create a multilink EtherChannel or VIF that is configured with multiple IP addresses. The number of IP addresses should be roughly equal to the number of VMNICs used for storage I/O in the ESX/ESXi hosts. This process is completed in the NSM.

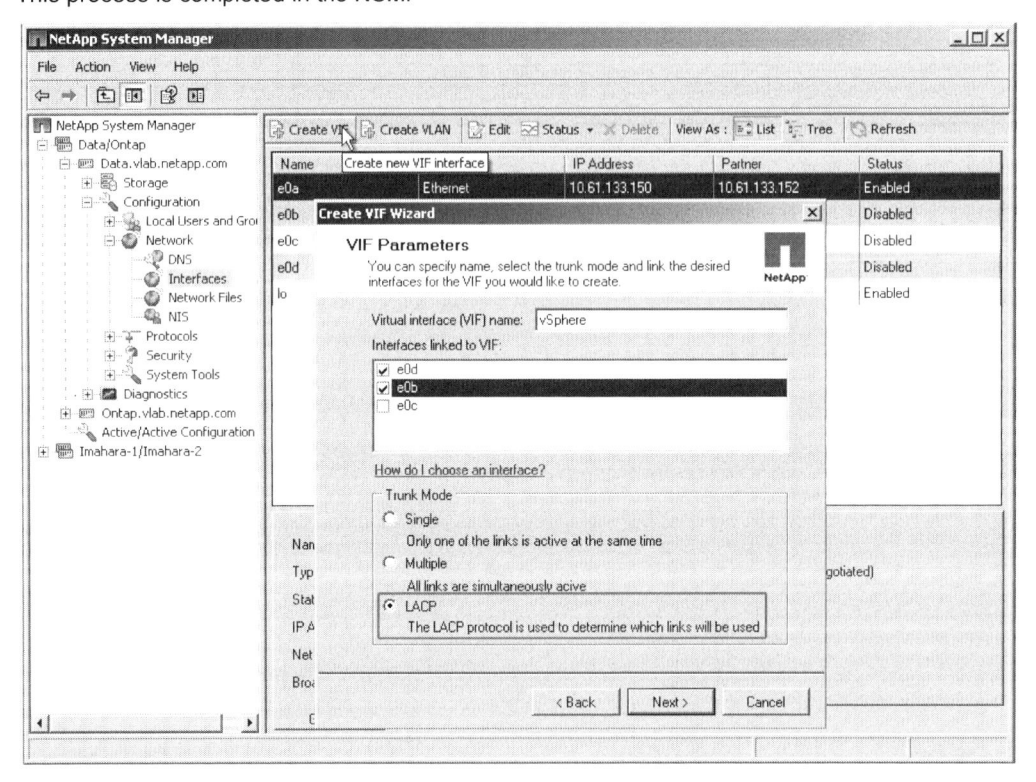

Figure 24) Creating an LACP EtherChannel port with two physical NICs on the first storage controller.

Note: There is one peculiar aspect when creating the first half of an EtherChannel on an HA storage array; when assigning the partner interface you have to select a physical NIC. The reason for this issue is there is no EtherChannel configured on the second storage controller. After the EtherChannel is configured, you have to return to the first and edit the partner interface for the EtherChannel created on the first controller.

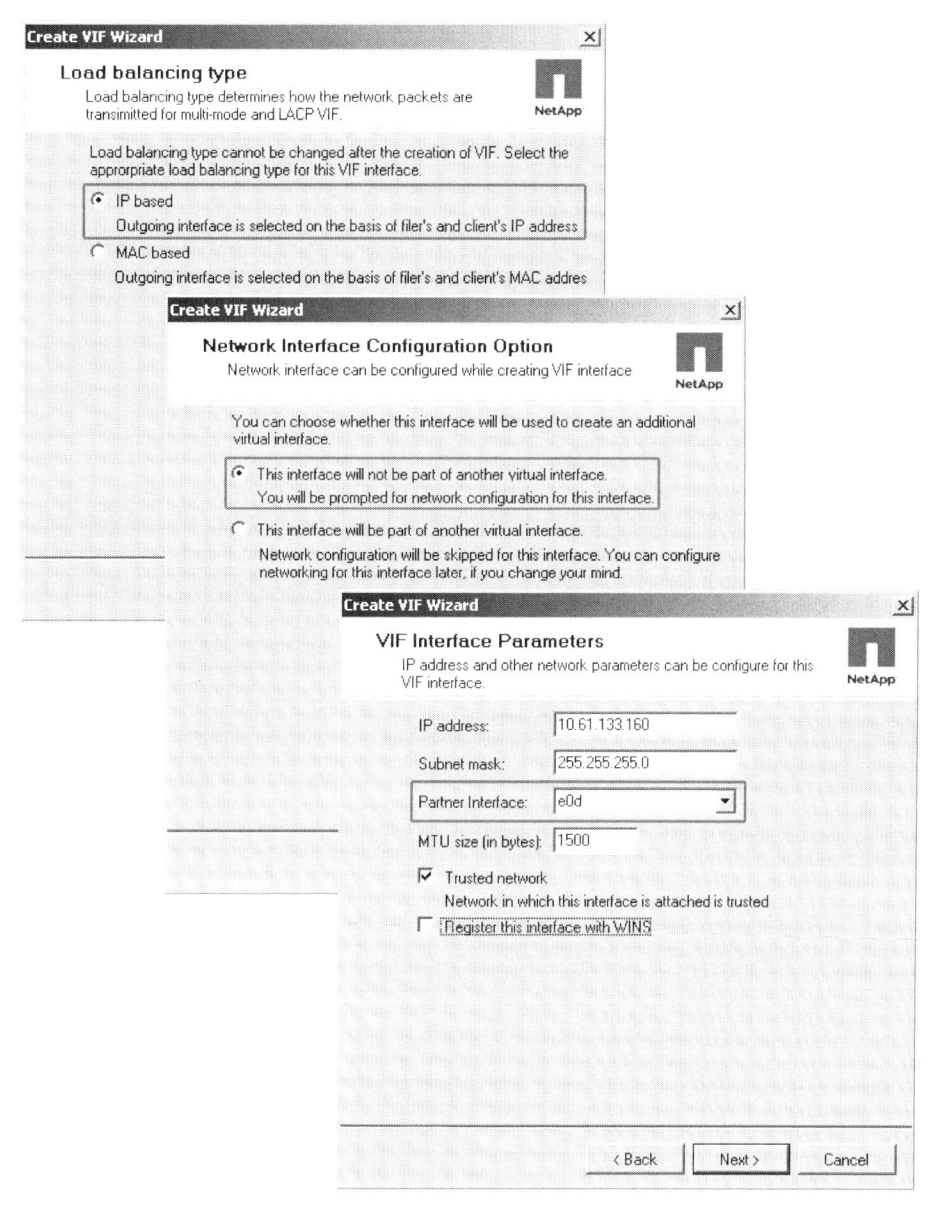

Figure 25) Completing the process of creating an LACP EtherChannel port with two physical NICs on the first storage controller.

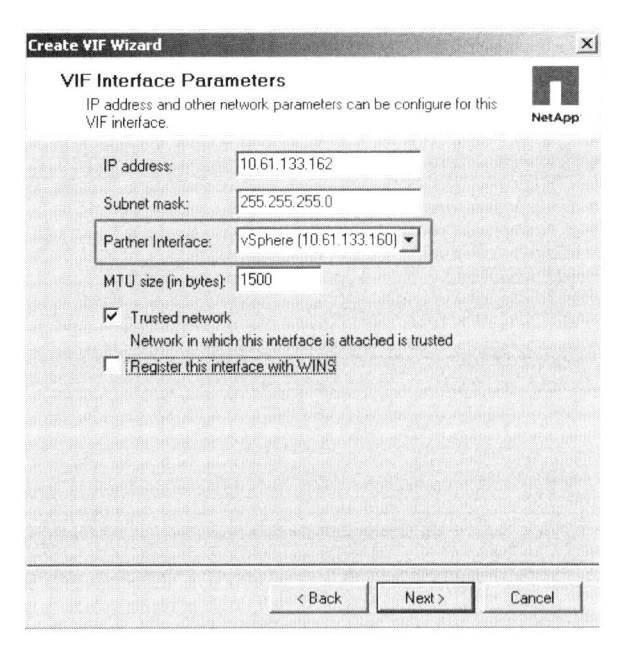

Figure 26) Completing the process of creating an LACP EtherChannel port with two physical NICs on the second storage controller. Notice the EtherChannel on the first controller is available to be selected as a partner interface.

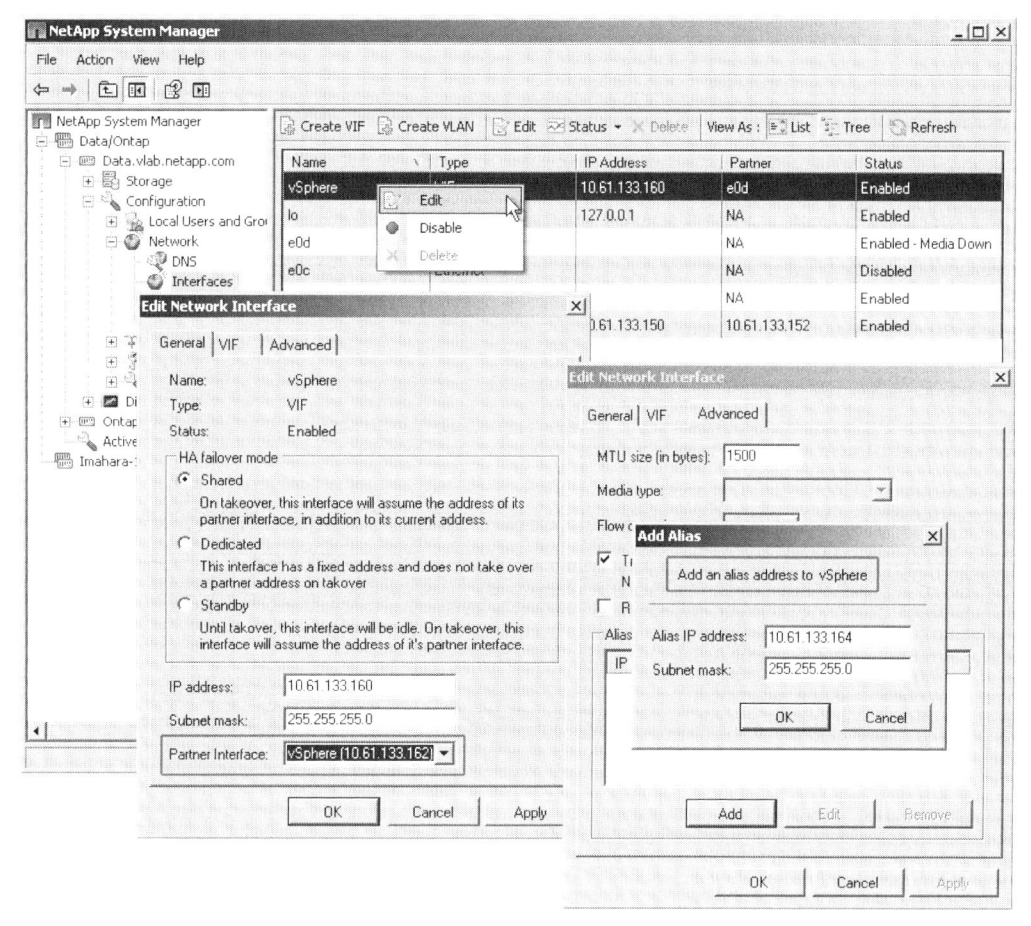

Figure 27) Completing the process of creating an LACP EtherChannel. On the first controller, the partner interface is set to the EtherChannel configured on the second array. Additional IP addresses can also be added by editing the EtherChannel.

CONFIGURING ESX/ESXI VMKERNEL STORAGE NETWORK PORTS

If the switches used for IP storage networking support multiswitch EtherChannel trunking or virtual port channeling, then each ESX server needs one physical connection to each switch in the stack with IP load balancing enabled. One VMkernel port with one IP address is required. Multiple datastore connections to the storage controller using different target IP addresses are necessary to use each of the available physical links.

ADVANTAGES

- Simple.
- Provides two active connections to each storage controller.
- Easily scales using more connections.
- Storage controller connection load balancing is automatically managed by IP load-balancing policy.
- Requires only one VMkernel port for IP storage to make use of multiple physical paths.

In the ESX server configuration shown in Figure 28, a vSwitch (named vSwitch1) has been created specifically for IP storage connectivity. Two physical adapters have been configured for this vSwitch (in this case vmnic1 and vmnic2). Each of these adapters is connected to a different physical switch, and the switch ports are configured into a cross-stack EtherChannel trunk.

Note: At this time, VMware does not support LACP, or IEEE 802.3ad, which is the dynamic negotiation of Ethernet trunks.

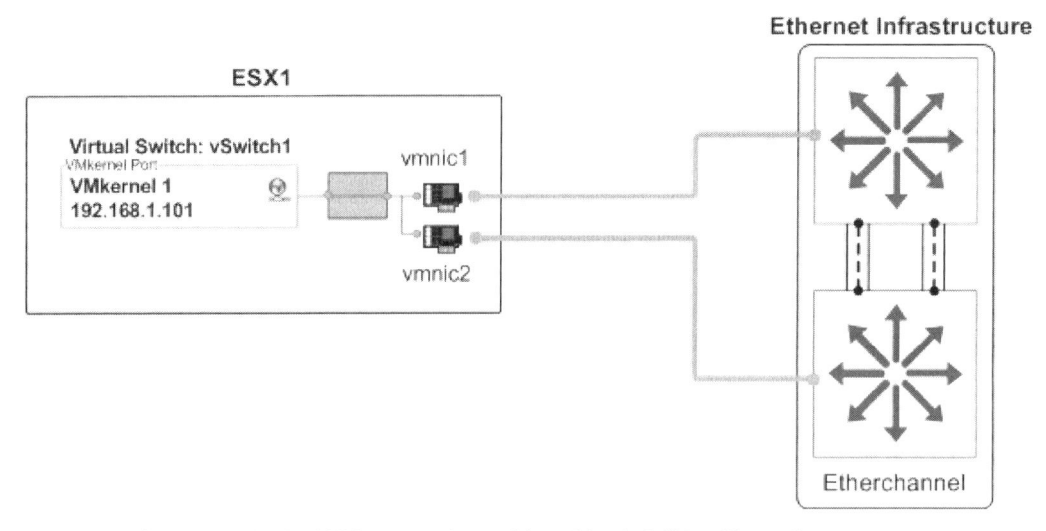

Figure 28) ESX server physical NIC connections with multiswitch EtherChannel.

In vSwitch1, one VMkernel port has been created (VMkernel 1) and configured with one IP address, and the NIC teaming properties of the VMkernel port have been configured as follows:

- **VMkernel 1:** IP address set to 192.168.1.101.
- **VMkernel 1 port properties:** Load-balancing policy set to "Route based on IP hash."

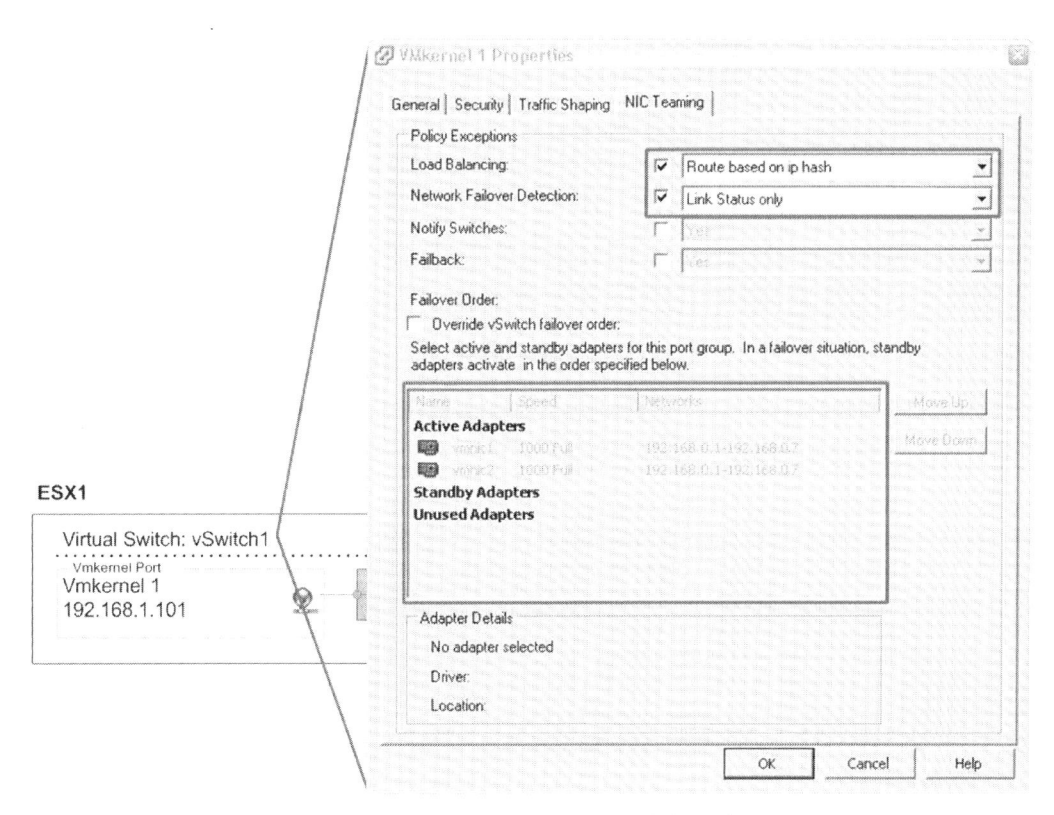

Figure 29) ESX server VMkernel port properties with multiswitch EtherChannel.

3.7   STORAGE NETWORK ARCHITECTURE WITH TRADITIONAL ETHERNET SWITCHES

In this configuration, the IP switches to be used do not support multiswitch link aggregation, so each storage controller requires four physical network connections. This design provides multiple active links to each storage controller, provides a means to scale throughput by simply adding more links, and requires multiple IP addresses per controller, and each uses two physical links for each active network connection in order to achieve path high availability.

THE SINGLE-MODE DESIGN

The single-mode design requires each pair of network links to be configured as a single-mode (active-passive) EtherChannel or VIF. Each VIF has a connection to both switches and has a single IP address assigned to it, providing two IP addresses on each controller. The `vif favor` command is used to force each VIF to use the appropriate switch for its active interface. This option is preferred due to its simplicity and the lack of any special configuration on the network switches.

ADVANTAGES OF USING SINGLE-MODE ETHERCHANNEL

- Simplicity: No switch-side configuration is required.
- Access from ESX/ESXi to datastore does not require multiswitch hop.

DISADVANTAGES OF USING SINGLE-MODE ETHERCHANNEL

Data I/O to a single IP is not aggregated over multiple links without adding more links.

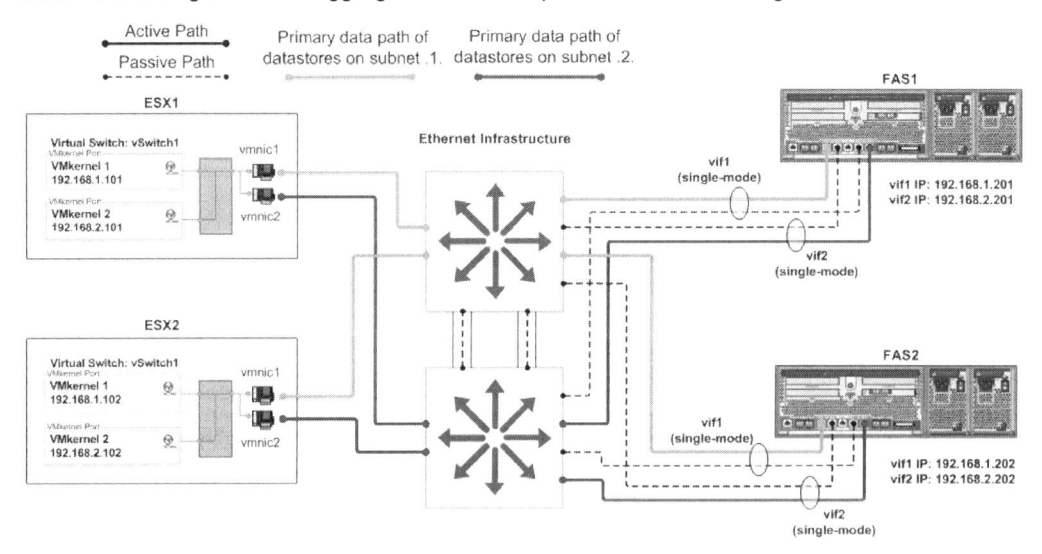

Figure 30) Storage side single-mode VIFs.

THE LAYERED MULTIMODE DESIGN

For customers preferring a layered multimode storage network architecture, we have included that network diagram in the appendix section of this document.

STORAGE LOAD BALANCING

Using multiple physical paths simultaneously on an IP storage network requires EtherChannel ports and multiple IP addresses on the storage controller and multiple VMkernel ports defined for storage I/O in the ESX/ESXi hosts. This model results in a design that balances datastore connectivity across all interfaces. This balancing is handled by the RCU at the time the datastore is provisioned.

MULTIPLE VMKERNEL PORTS

The use of multiple VMkernel ports is a defined standard method developed by NetApp and repeated by other storage vendors offering arrays with multiprotocol access. NetApp recommends defining a separate VMkernel for each storage protocol. Doing so makes the configuration of iSCSI with NFS very simple. Each of these VMkernel ports supports IP traffic on a different subnet. Using different subnet addressing schemes for iSCSI and NFS provides the benefit of being able to control which VMkernel ports are used for communication of each protocol. As an example, see Figure 31. Because the two VMkernel ports are in the same vSwitch, they can share the vmnics in a vSwitch.

For NFS datastores, each VMkernel port is configured with a single active vmnic, with one or more standby vmnics defined. This allows the administrator to control which vmnic is used for traffic by each VMkernel port.

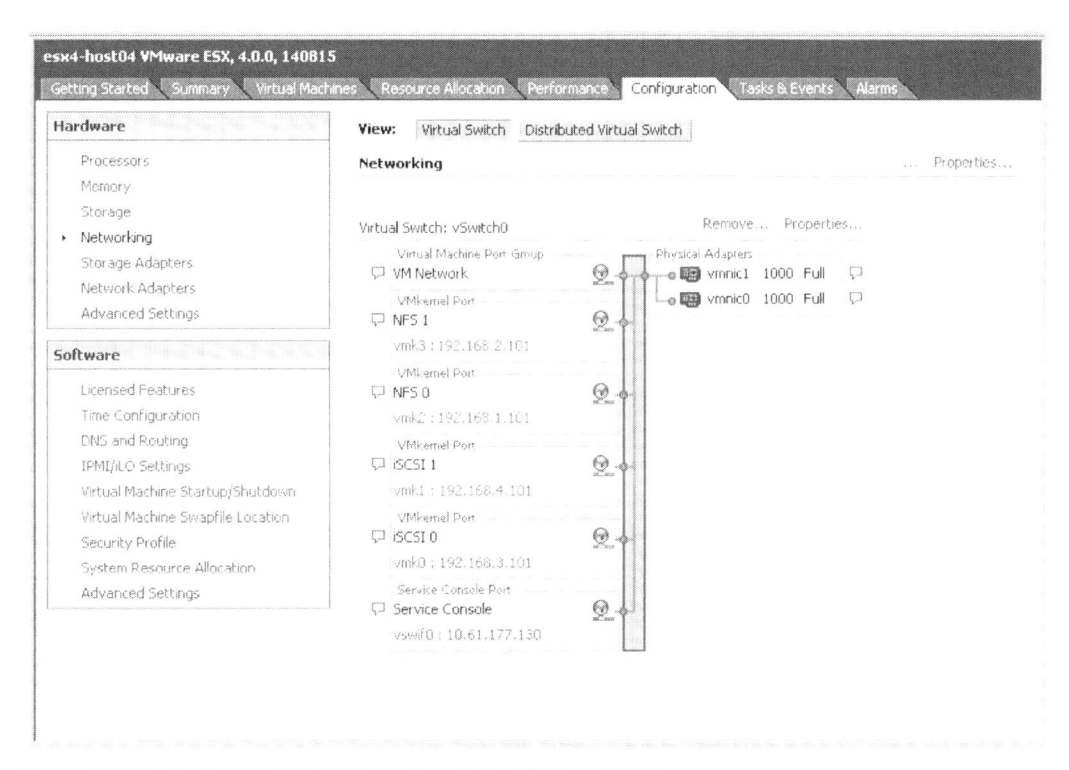

Figure 31) Displaying multiple VMkernel ports for iSCSI and NFS.

Figure 32 shows an overview of storage traffic flow when using multiple ESX servers and multiple datastores.

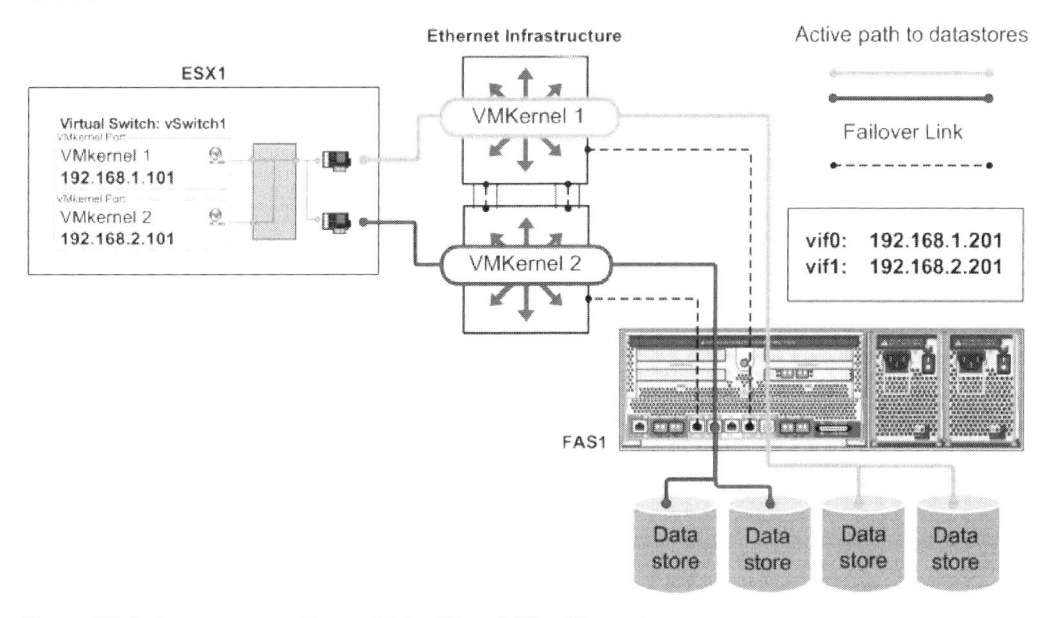

Figure 32) Datastore connections with traditional EtherChannel.

ESX SERVER ADAPTER FAILOVER BEHAVIOR WITH ISCSI

In case of ESX server adapter failure (due to a cable pull or NIC failure), traffic originally running over the failed adapter is rerouted and continues using the second adapter. This failover is managed by VMware native multipathing, thus, there is no need for network failover configuration on the switch or VMkernel. Traffic returns to the original adapter when service to the adapter is restored.

ESX SERVER ADAPTER FAILOVER BEHAVIOR WITH NFS

In case of ESX server adapter failure (due to a cable pull or NIC failure), traffic originally running over the failed adapter is rerouted and continues using the second adapter, but on the same subnet where it originated. Both subnets are now active on the surviving physical adapter. Traffic returns to the original adapter when service to the adapter is restored. In this scenario EtherChannel provides the network failover.

SWITCH FAILURE

Traffic originally running to the failed switch is rerouted and continues using the other available adapter, through the surviving switch, to the NetApp storage controller. Traffic returns to the original adapter when the failed switch is repaired or replaced.

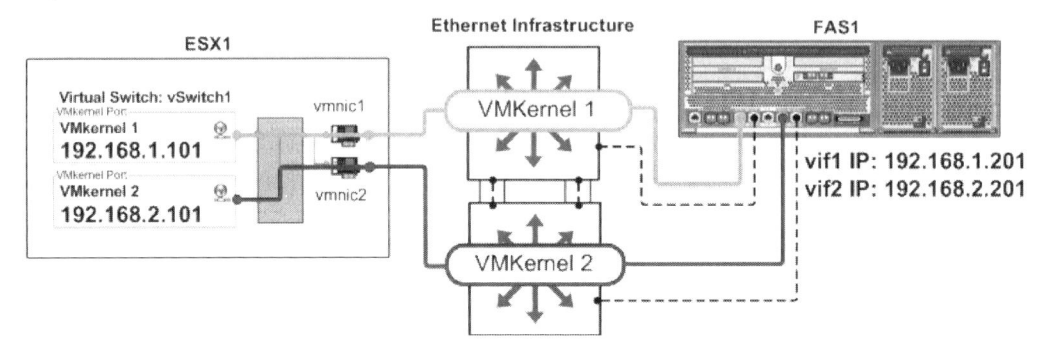

Figure 33) ESX vSwitch1 normal mode operation.

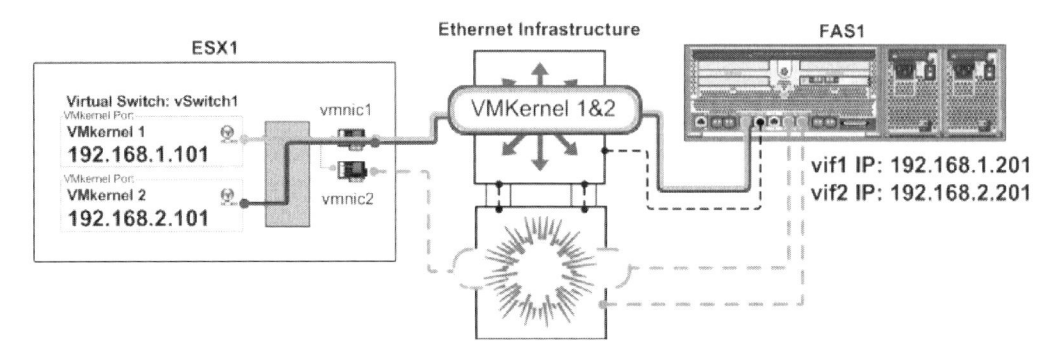

Figure 34) ESX vSwitch failover mode operation.

CONFIGURING NETAPP STORAGE NETWORK PORTS

If your plans are to deploy with IP-based storage access, NFS, or iSCSI, then you need to configure multiple Ethernet links to operate together as an EtherChannel. EtherChannel provides aggregated bandwidth and link availability from the network switches to the storage controller.

This design is recommended, because the storage controller handles the aggregated I/O load from all ESX/ESXI nodes.

NetApp supports all modes of EtherChannels, which are compliant with 802.3ad LACP, and/or static EtherChannels. In Data ONTAP EtherChannels are referred to as virtual interfaces (VIFs). NetApp recommends that you configure your EtherChannel or VIFs as single mode with traditional switches, because this is the simplest network architecture.

For use in a traditional switch configuration, you need to create a single-mode EtherChannel or VIF that is configured with a single IP address. This process is completed in the NSM.

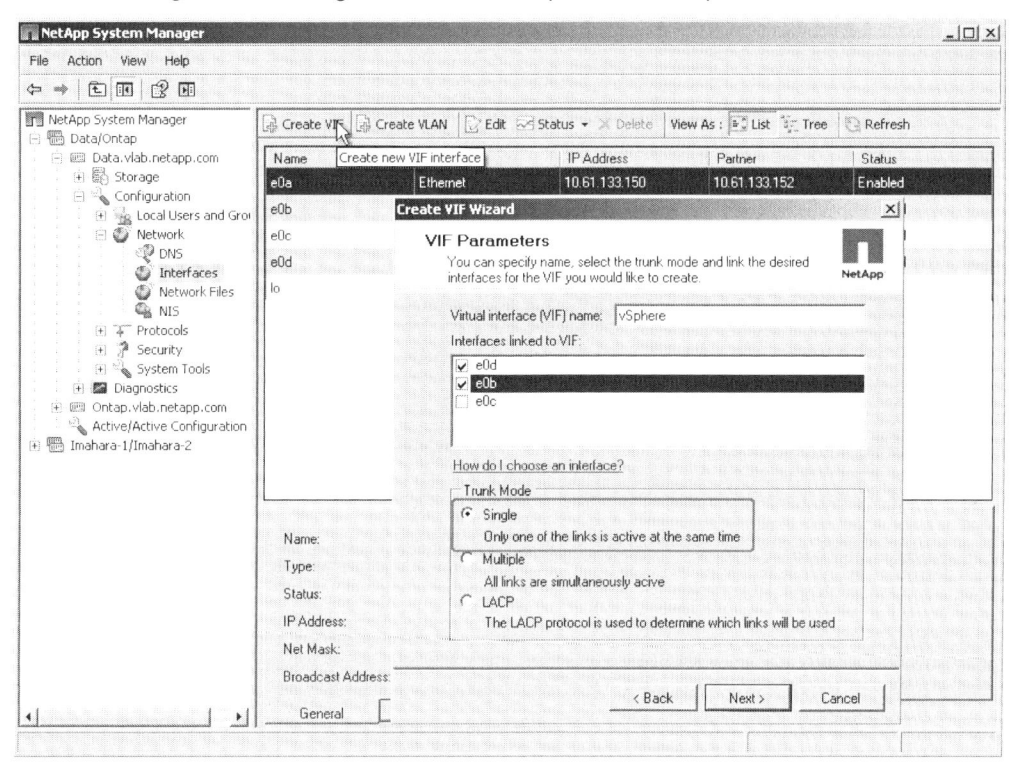

Figure 35) Creating an LACP EtherChannel port with two physical NICs on the first storage controller.

Note: There is one peculiar aspect when creating the first half of an EtherChannel on an HA storage array; when assigning the partner interface, you have to select a physical NIC. The reason for this issue is there is no EtherChannel configured on the second storage controller. After the EtherChannel is configured, you must return to the first and edit the partner interface for the EtherChannel created on the first controller.

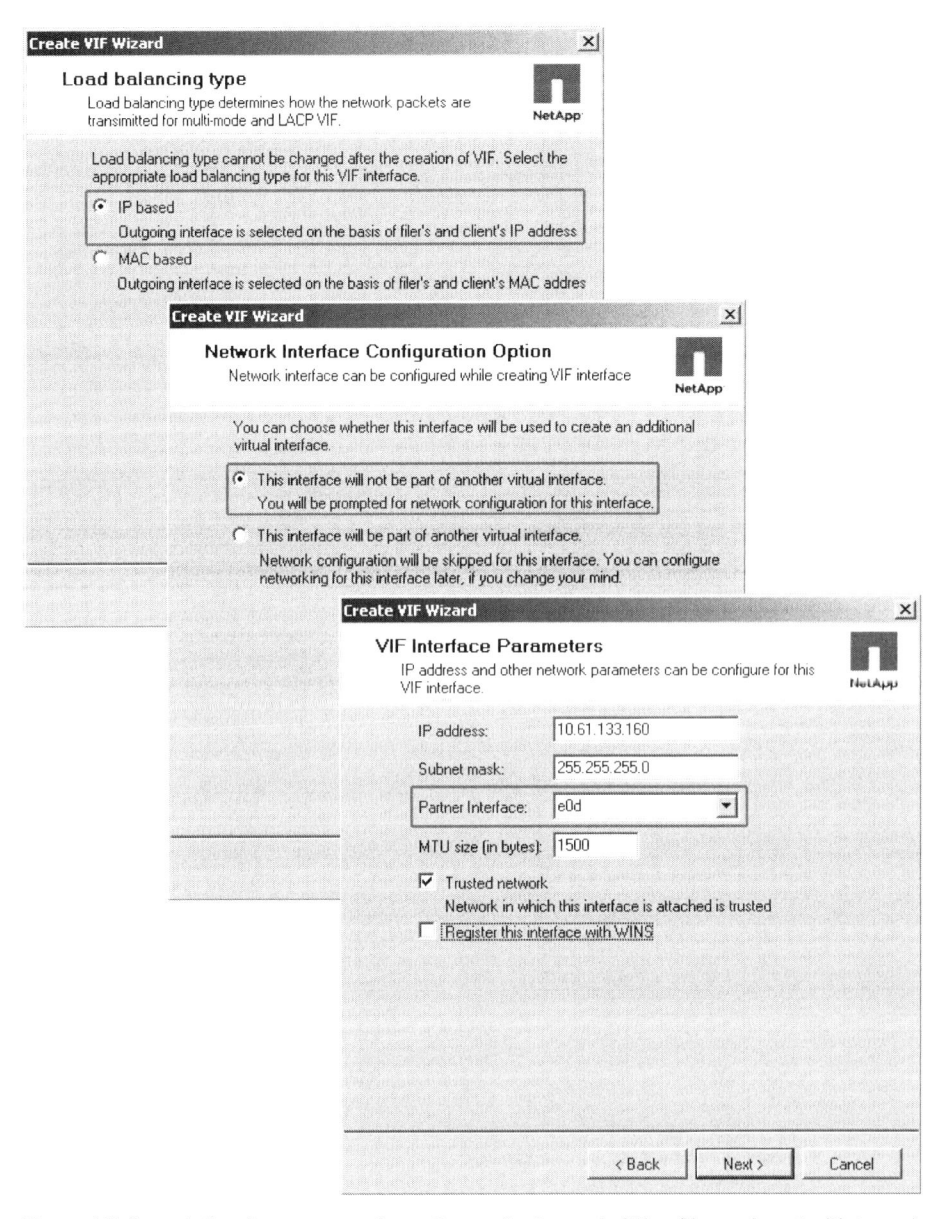

Figure 36) Completing the process of creating a single-mode EtherChannel port with two physical NICs on the first storage controller.

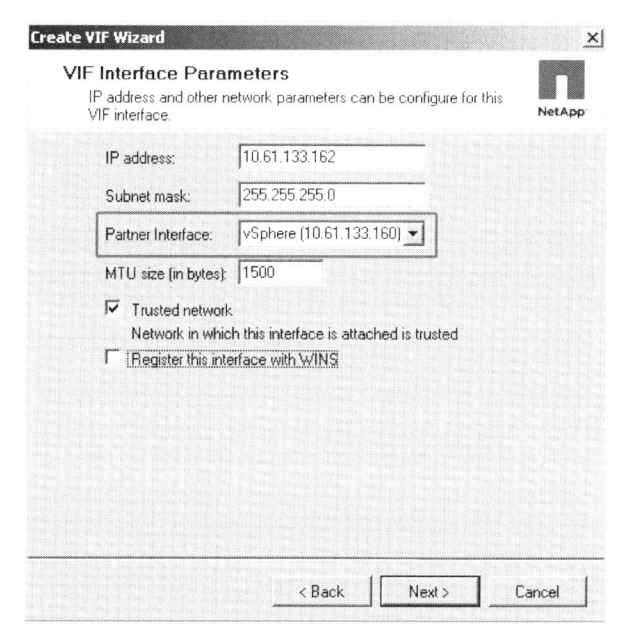

Figure 37) Completing the process of creating a single-mode EtherChannel port with two physical NICs on the second storage controller. Notice the EtherChannel on the first controller is available to be selected as a partner interface.

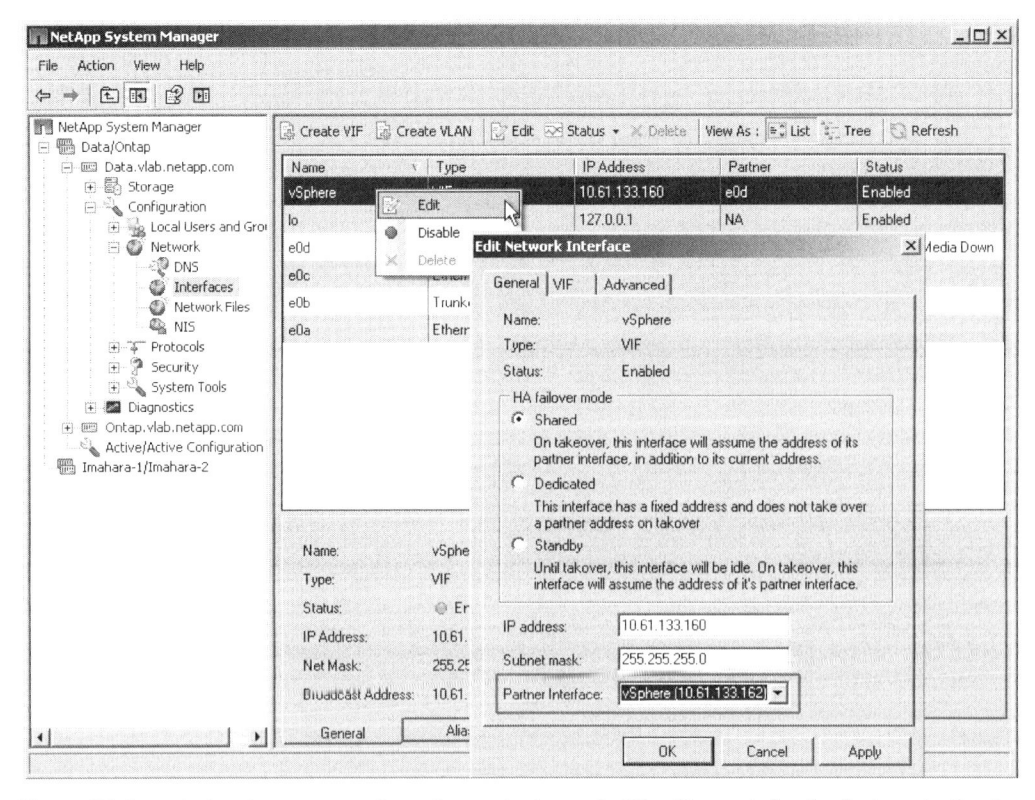

Figure 38) Completing the process of creating a single-mode EtherChannel. On the first controller the partner interface is set to the EtherChannel configured on the second array.

CONFIGURING ESX/ESXI VMKERNEL STORAGE NETWORK PORTS

With traditional storage switches each ESX/ESXi hosts must be configured with at least two VMkernel IP storage ports addressed on different subnets. As with the previous option, multiple datastore connections to the storage controller are necessary using different target IP addresses. Without the addition of a second VMkernel port, the VMkernel would simply route all outgoing requests through the same physical interface, without making use of additional vmnics on the vSwitch. In this configuration, each VMkernel port is set with its IP address on a different subnet. The target storage system is also configured with IP addresses on each of those subnets, so the use of specific vmnic interfaces can be controlled.

ADVANTAGES

- Provides two active connections to each storage controller (but only one active path per datastore).
- Easily scales to more connections.
- Storage controller connection load balancing is automatically managed virtual port load-balancing policy. This is a non-EtherChannel solution.

DISADVANTAGE

- Requires the configuration of at least two VMkernel IP storage ports.

In the ESX/ESXi host configuration shown in Figure 39, a vSwitch (named vSwitch1) has been created specifically for IP storage connectivity. Two physical adapters have been configured for this vSwitch (in this case, vmnic1 and vmnic2). Each of these adapters is connected to a different physical switch.

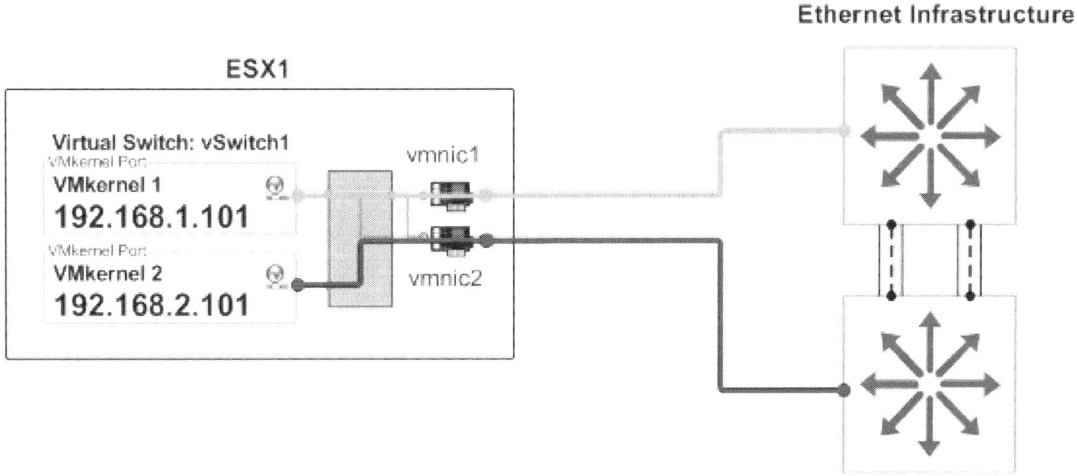

Figure 39) ESX server physical NIC connections with traditional Ethernet.

In vSwitch1, two VMkernel ports have been created (VMkernel 1 and VMkernel 2). Each VMkernel port has been configured with an IP address on a different subnet, and the NIC teaming properties of each VMkernel port have been configured as follows.

- **VMkernel 1:** IP address set to 192.168.1.101.
- **VMkernel 1 port properties:**
    - Enable the override vSwitch failover order option.
    - For NFS and iSCSI, set active adapter to vmnic1.
    - For NFS, set standby adapter to vmnic2.
    - For iSCSI, set other adapters to unused.
- **VMkernel 2:** IP address set to 192.168.2.101.
- **VMkernel2 port properties:**
    - Enable the override vSwitch failover order option.
    - For NFS and iSCSI, set active adapter to vmnic2.
    - For NFS, set standby adapter to vmnic1.
    - For iSCSI, set other adapters to unused.

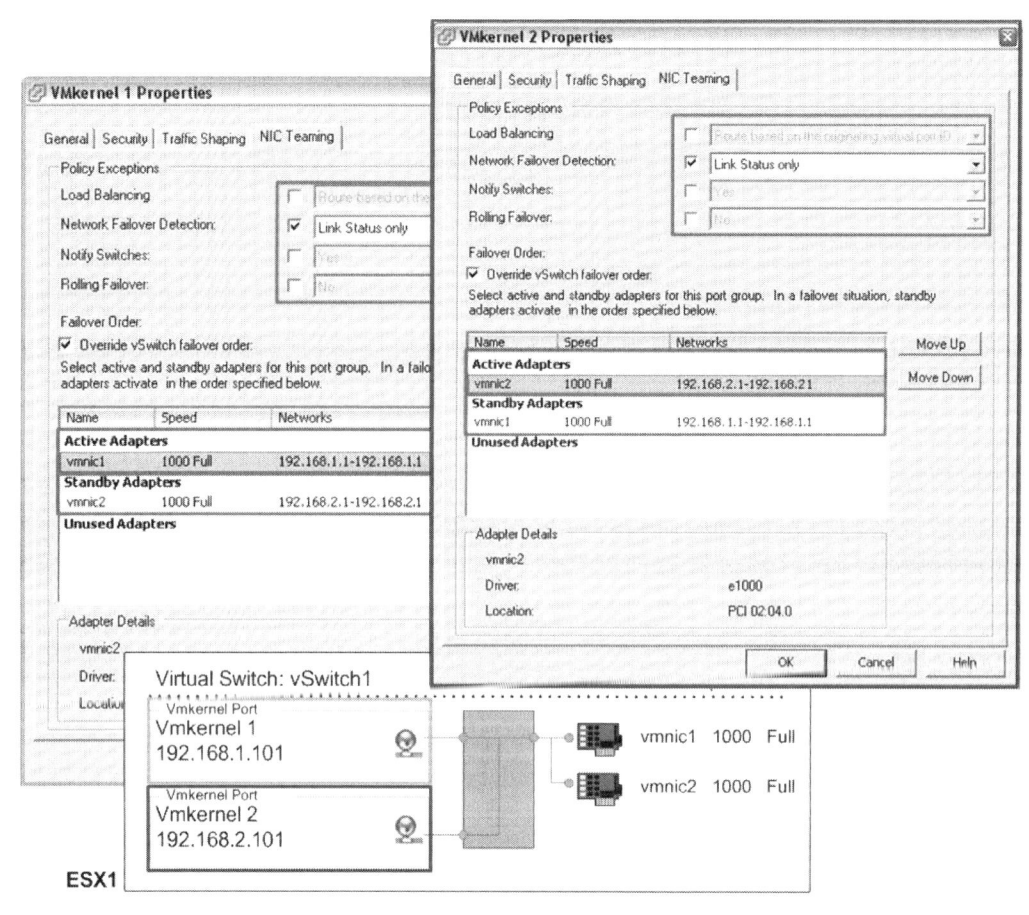

Figure 40) ESX server VMkernel port properties with traditional Ethernet.

3.8 ENABLING MULTIPLE TCP SESSION SUPPORT FOR ISCSI

With vSphere you have the option to enable the use of multiple TCP sessions with iSCSI. This feature enables round robin load balancing using VMware native multipathing and requires a VMkernel port to be defined for each vmnic assigned to iSCSI traffic.

For iSCSI datastores, each VMkernel port is configured with a single vmnic. No standby vmnics may exist in the VMkernel.

Note: Configuring iSCSI VMkernel ports as described in this section results in the individual iSCSI VMkernel ports being configured without NIC teaming and therefore no network layer redundancy. In this configuration, iSCSI redundancy is provided by the native multipathing layer in ESX/ESXi. In this way, iSCSI redundancy is provided in the same way as FC redundancy. Enabling multiple TCP session support for iSCSI on ESX/ESXi hosts that also connect with NFS is not supported and should not be done, because it might result in NFS mounts occurring over the iSCSI VMkernel ports, which have no network layer redundancy. NetApp recommends that hosts requiring the concurrent use of both iSCSI and NFS rely on the TCP layer of the network using NIC teaming for storage path redundancy, as described in the previous sections.

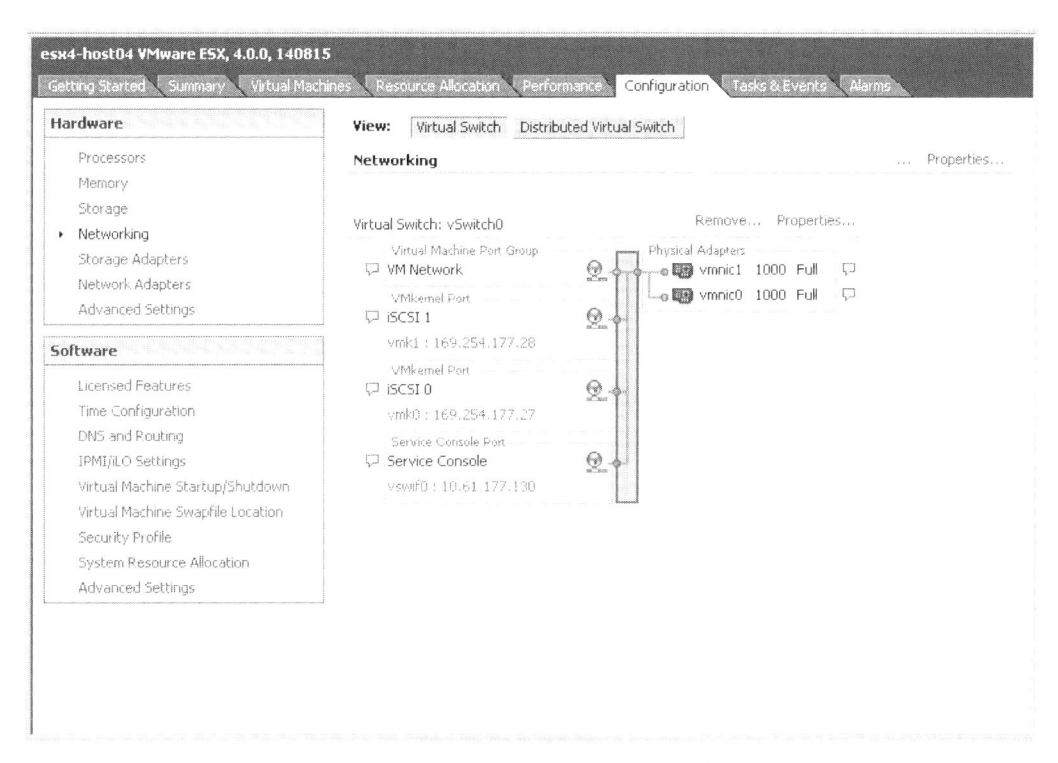

Figure 41) Displaying multiple VMkernel ports for iSCSI with support for multiple TCP sessions.

Note: ESX/ESXi 4 supports a maximum of four iSCSI ports per host.

CREATE MULTIPLE ISCSI VMKERNELS TO SUPPORT MULTIPLE TCP SESSIONS WITH ISCSI

1. Open vCenter Server.
2. Select an ESX host.
3. In the right pane, select the Configuration tab.
4. In the Hardware box, select Networking.
5. In the upper-right corner, click Add Networking to open the Add Network wizard.
6. Select the VMkernel radio button and click Next.

   Note: You will create a VMkernel for every Ethernet link that you want to dedicate to iSCSI traffic. Note that VMkernels can be on different IP subnets.

7. Configure the VMkernel by providing the required network information. A default gateway is not required for the VMkernel IP storage network.
8. Each VMkernel must be configured to use a single active adapter that is not used by any other iSCSI VMkernel. Also, each VMkernel must not have any standby adapters. See Figure 42 and Figure 43.

   The software iSCSI daemon is required to be bound to each VMkernel. This step can only be completed using the CLI.

9. Connect to an ESX or ESXi console and run the following:

   ```
   esxcli swiscsi nic add -n <VMkernel ID> -d <Virtual HBA ID>
   ```

As an example:

```
esxcli swiscsi nic add -n vmk0 -d vmhba33
esxcli swiscsi nic add -n vmk1 -d vmhba33
```

10. Verify the iSCSI-to-VMkernel bindings. Connect to an ESX or ESXi console and run the following:

```
esxcli swiscsi nic list -d <Virtual HBA ID>
```

As an example:

```
esxcli swiscsi nic list -d vmhba33
```

See Figure 44.

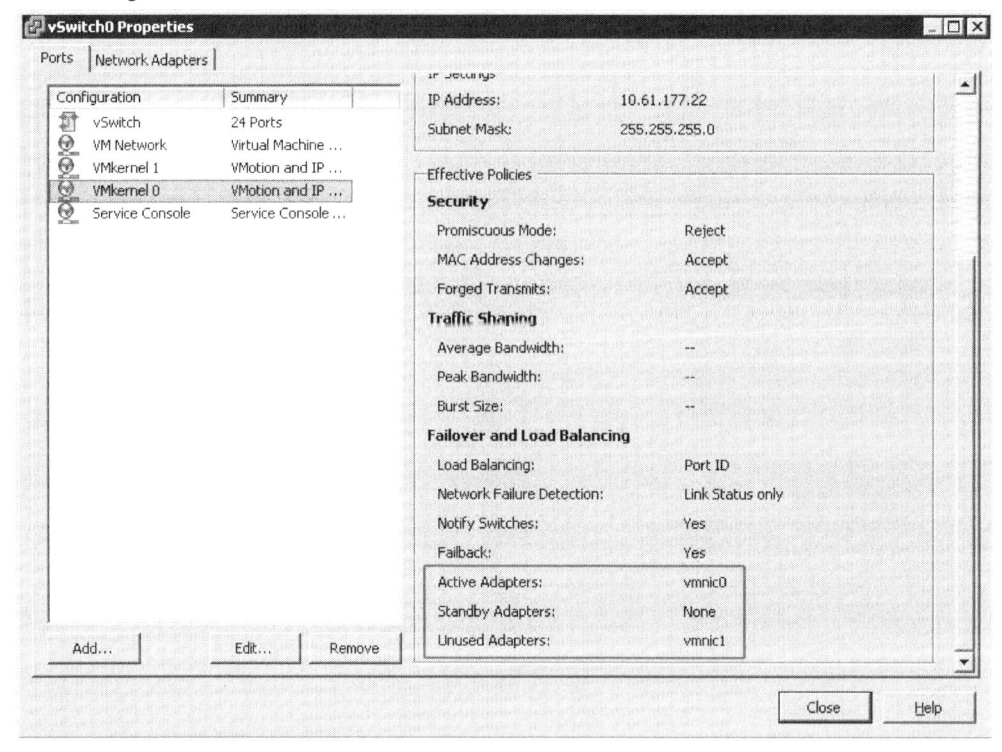

Figure 42) iSCSI VMkernel 0: Note active adapter vmnic0.

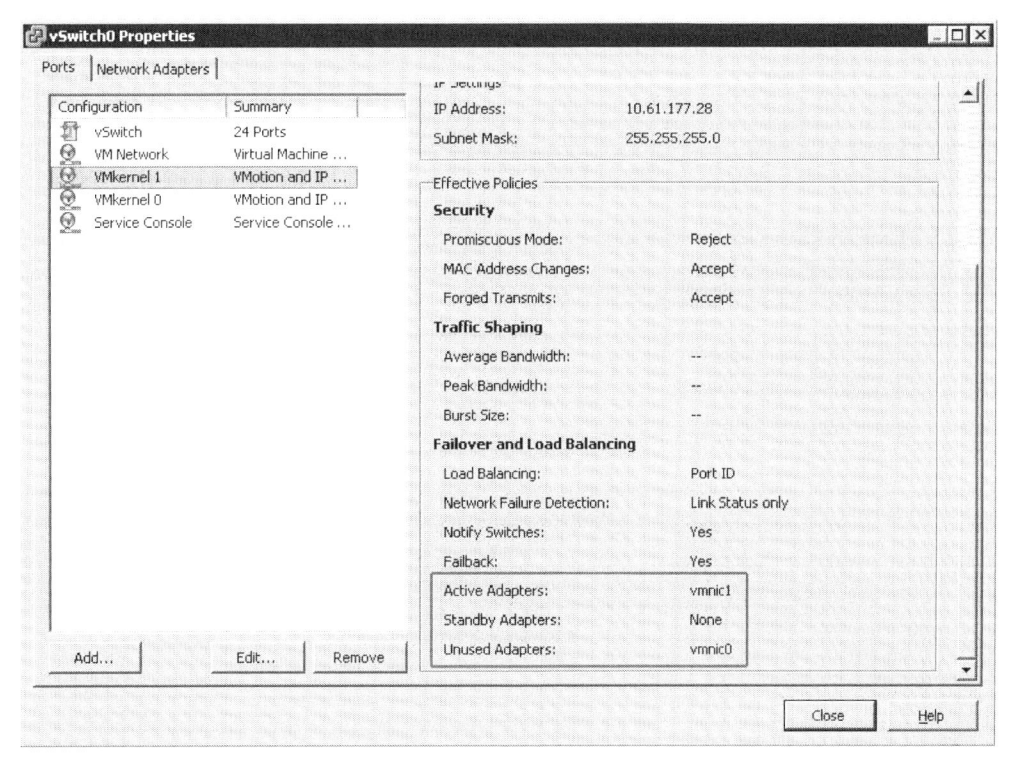

Figure 43) iSCSI VMkernel 1: Note active adapter vmnic1.

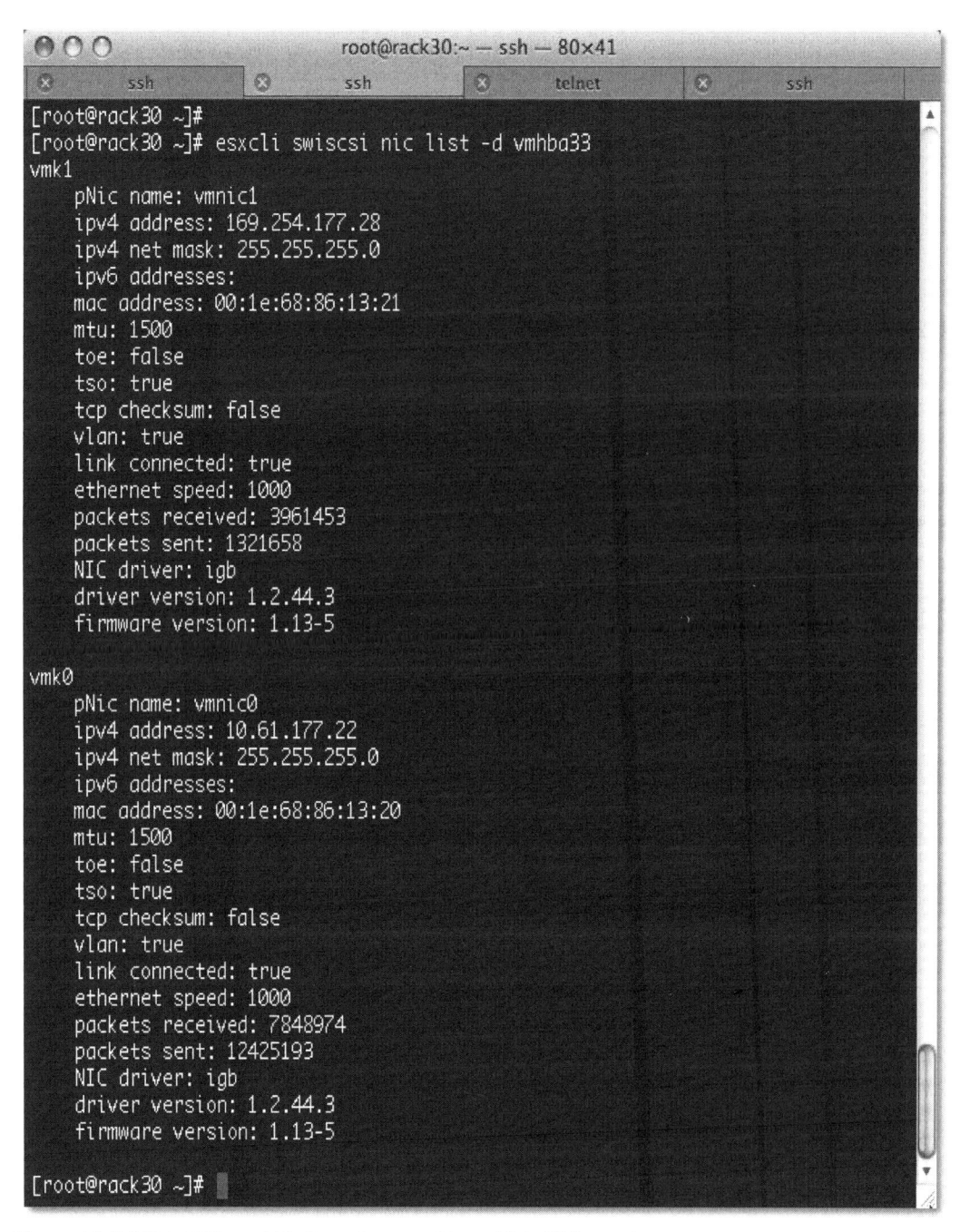

```
[root@rack30 ~]#
[root@rack30 ~]# esxcli swiscsi nic list -d vmhba33
vmk1
    pNic name: vmnic1
    ipv4 address: 169.254.177.28
    ipv4 net mask: 255.255.255.0
    ipv6 addresses:
    mac address: 00:1e:68:86:13:21
    mtu: 1500
    toe: false
    tso: true
    tcp checksum: false
    vlan: true
    link connected: true
    ethernet speed: 1000
    packets received: 3961453
    packets sent: 1321658
    NIC driver: igb
    driver version: 1.2.44.3
    firmware version: 1.13-5

vmk0
    pNic name: vmnic0
    ipv4 address: 10.61.177.22
    ipv4 net mask: 255.255.255.0
    ipv6 addresses:
    mac address: 00:1e:68:86:13:20
    mtu: 1500
    toe: false
    tso: true
    tcp checksum: false
    vlan: true
    link connected: true
    ethernet speed: 1000
    packets received: 7848974
    packets sent: 12425193
    NIC driver: igb
    driver version: 1.2.44.3
    firmware version: 1.13-5

[root@rack30 ~]#
```

Figure 44) iSCSI to VMkernel bindings for use with multiple TCP sessions.

4 STORAGE ARRAY DESIGN AND SETUP

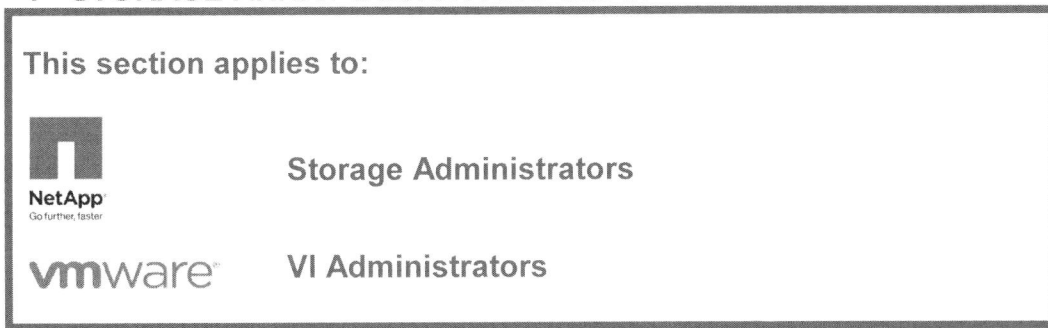

This section applies to:

Storage Administrators

VI Administrators

4.1 A NEW OPERATIONAL MODEL: PROVISIONING RESOURCE POOLS

The technologies available from NetApp and covered in this document provide the means for a new operational model where storage administrators can significantly simplify their support for virtual infrastructures.

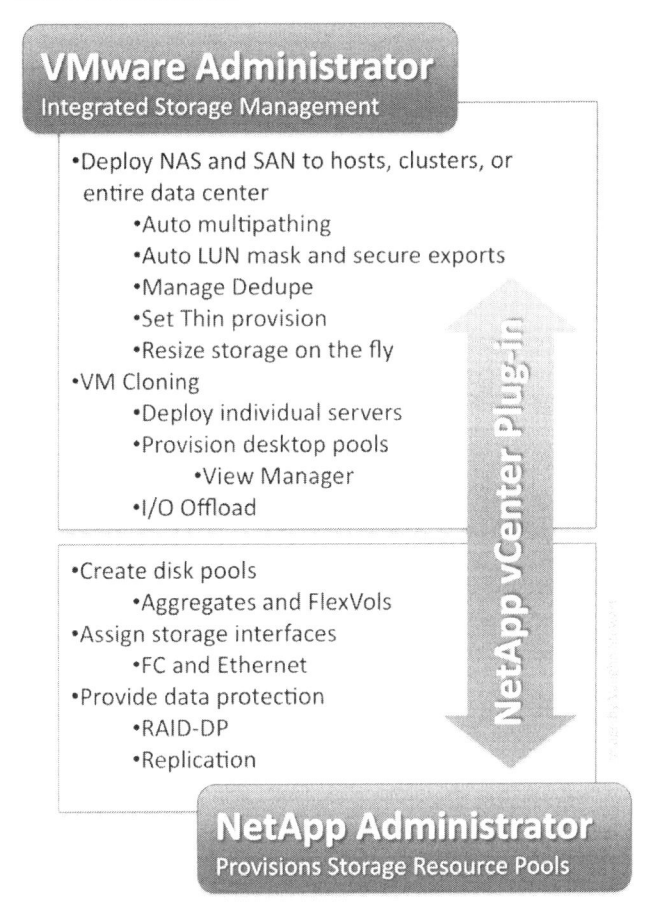

Figure 45) NetApp vCenter plug-in responsibilities.

In this new model, storage admins are responsible for configuring the physical storage array enabling data protection and storage connectivity. Once the physical architecture is deployed, NetApp admins supporting VMware can simply provision pools of "raw" storage resources (aggregates, FlexVol volumes, and storage network interfaces) directly for use in the virtual infrastructure.

This model significantly simplifies the tasks required by the storage admin while allowing the VMware admin to provision and manage datastores and the storage constructs associated with them such as LUN masking, storage I/O path management, and so on directly from physical resources assigned to the virtual infrastructure by the NetApp admin.

This design does not prohibit an IT staff from deploying and managing storage in a traditional manner, which might be described as one where the storage admin creates specific storage objects and the VMware administrative team connects to and uses these objects.

We trust all admin teams within a virtual data center will benefit from the use of our VMware integration in order to run their business more simply and with a higher degree of efficiency. In NetApp terms, "go further, faster."

NETAPP VCENTER PLUG-INS

The NetApp vCenter plug-ins, the Virtual Storage Console (VSC) and the Rapid Cloning Utility (RCU), have been combined into one NetApp plug-in framework with the release of the VSC version 2.0. Additionally, the VSC 2.0 now includes access to all the capabilities of the NetApp SnapManager for Virtual Infrastructure (SMVI) product directly in the vSphere client interface.

The VSC nondisruptively sets storage-related configurations to their recommended values on ESX/ESXi hosts. In addition, the VSC 2.0 provides automated provisioning of storage resource pools as datastores in a dynamic means by the VMware administrators. This provisioning model configures all storage access to follow NetApp recommended best practices in terms of availability, access control, and storage path management.

4.2   STORAGE ARCHITECTURE CONCEPTS

Before you begin configuring your storage array for running a virtual infrastructure, make sure you have the following information prepared in advance:

1. Separate networks for storage array management and storage I/O. This concept applies to all storage protocols but is very pertinent to Ethernet-based deployments (NFS, iSCSI, FCoE). The separation can be physical (subnets) or logical (VLANs), but must exist.

2. If leveraging an IP-based storage protocol I/O (NFS or iSCSI), you might require more than a single IP address for the storage target. The determination is based on the capabilities of your networking hardware.

3. With IP-based storage protocols (NFS and iSCSI) you channel multiple Ethernet ports together. NetApp refers to this function as a VIF. It is recommended that you create LACP VIFs over multimode VIFs whenever possible.

4.3   NETAPP STORAGE CONSTRUCTS

A byproduct of any consolidation effort is increased risk if the consolidation platform fails. As physical servers are converted to virtual machines and multiple VMs are consolidated onto a single physical platform, the impact of a failure to the single platform could be catastrophic. Fortunately, VMware provides multiple technologies that enhance availability of a virtual data center. These technologies include increased VM availability and load balancing with VMware HA and DRS clustering, zero-loss application availability with fault tolerance, and the ability to nondisruptively migrate running VMs and their datasets between physical ESX servers with VMotion and storage VMotion, respectively.

When focusing on storage availability, many levels of redundancy are available for deployments, including purchasing physical servers with multiple storage interconnects or HBAs, deploying redundant storage networking and network paths, and leveraging storage arrays with redundant controllers. A deployed storage design that meets all of these criteria can be considered to have eliminated all single points of failure.

DATA PROTECTION AND RAID-DP

The reality is that data protection requirements in a virtual infrastructure are greater than those in a traditional physical server infrastructure. Data protection is a paramount feature of shared storage devices. NetApp RAID-DP® is an advanced RAID technology that is provided as the default RAID level on all FAS systems. RAID-DP protects against the simultaneous loss of two drives in a single RAID group. It is very economical to deploy; the overhead with default RAID groups is a mere 12.5%. This level of resiliency and storage efficiency makes data residing on RAID-DP safer than data stored on RAID 5 and more cost effective than RAID 10. NetApp recommends using RAID-DP on all RAID groups that store VMware data.

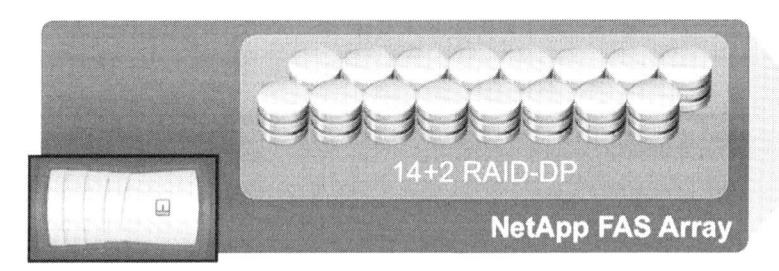

Figure 46) NetApp RAID-DP.

AGGREGATES

An aggregate is NetApp's virtualization layer, which abstracts physical disks from logical datasets that are referred to as *flexible volumes.* Aggregates are the means by which the total IOPS available to all of the physical disks are pooled as a resource. This design is well suited to meet the needs of an unpredictable and mixed workload.

NetApp controllers store their files required to run the array on a root aggregate. Whenever possible, NetApp recommends you use a dedicated two-disk aggregate. By default the root aggregate is composed of three disks due to the overhead of RAID-DP. To reduce the disk total from three to two, you must modify the RAID type from RAID-DP to RAID-4. Note that this recommendation is very difficult to implement when you have a small number of disk drives. In these scenarios, it is probably best to not deploy with a dedicated root aggregate.

The remaining storage should be placed into a small number of large aggregates. The overall disk I/O from VMware environments is traditionally random by nature, so this storage design gives optimal performance because a large number of physical spindles are available to service I/O requests. On smaller FAS arrays, it might not be practical to have more than a single aggregate, due to the restricted number of disk drives on the system. In these cases, it is acceptable to have only a single aggregate.

FLEXIBLE VOLUMES

Flexible volumes contain either LUNs or virtual disk files that are accessed by VMware ESX servers.

NetApp recommends a one-to-one relationship between VMware datastores and flexible volumes when deploying virtual servers. For virtual desktops NetApp recommends a one-to-one relationship between VMware desktop pools and flexible volumes.

This design offers an easy means to understand the VMware data layout when viewing the storage configuration from the FAS array. This mapping model also makes it easy to implement Snapshot backups and SnapMirror replication policies at the datastore level, because NetApp implements these storage-side features at the flexible volume level.

LUNS

LUNs are units of SCSI addressed (FC, iSCSI, and FCoE) storage that when connected to an ESX/ESXi cluster, are used as a shared VMFS datastore or raw device mapping (RDM). For more information, see the VMware Storage/SAN Compatibility Guide for ESX/ESXi.

STORAGE NAMING CONVENTIONS

NetApp storage systems allow human or canonical naming conventions. In a well-planned virtual infrastructure implementation, a descriptive naming convention aids in identification and mapping through the multiple layers of virtualization from storage to the virtual machines. A simple and efficient naming convention also facilitates configuration of replication and disaster recovery processes.

NetApp suggests the following naming guidelines:

- **Name of aggregate:** Can be any name the storage admin selects.
- **Name of FlexVol volume:** Should match the name of the datastore.
- **LUN name for VMFS:** Should match the name of the datastore.
- **LUN name for RDMs:** Should include both the hostname and volume label or name.

4.4   NETAPP ARRAY CONFIGURATION

In this section we will walk through the steps required to configure and provision a NetApp storage array into physical resource pools.

NETAPP SYSTEMS MANAGER

NetApp provides the NetApp Systems Manager (NSM) as a convenient means to deploy a new storage array or manage a moderate number of storage arrays. There are additional methods to manage storage arrays powered by Data ONTAP, which include legacy array-based methods such as FilerView® and the command line interface (CLI) all the up to global monitoring and management using Operations Manager.

In this document we use the NSM exclusively for array-based configuration by the storage administrative team. We have included the traditional configuration steps from earlier versions of this document in the appendix section.

DISCOVERING ARRAYS POWERED BY DATA ONTAP

Begin by downloading and installing the NSM from NOW™ onto a server or virtual machine based on Windows. Rack and cable your NetApp array. You are required to connect at least one Ethernet port in order to complete a network-based setup that requires the assignment of a temporary IP address using DHCP. Alternatively, you can connect a serial cable to the array and complete the command line setup wizard that launches at power on.

In either scenario you can launch the NSM and allow it to autodiscover your storage arrays by entering either the array's IP address or the IP subnet on which the array resides. For more information on setting up a new array using the NSM, refer to the NetApp Systems Manager Quick Start Guide.

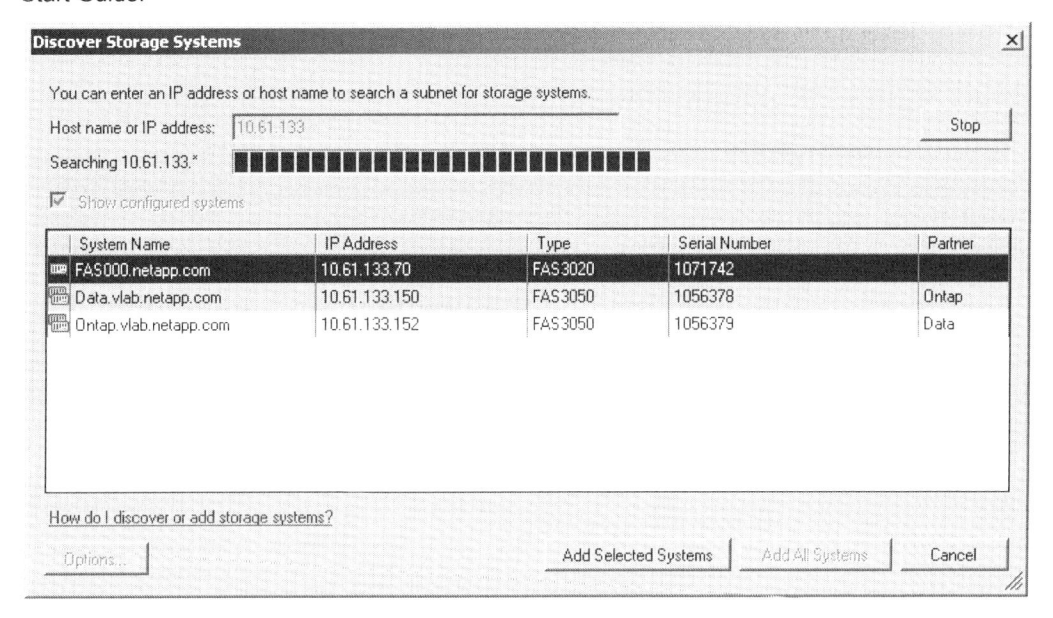

Figure 47) Discovering arrays using NetApp Systems Manager.

CONFIGURING STORAGE NETWORK INTERFACES

If you are planning on deploying a FC or FCoE configuration, nothing is required to configure on the storage array other than enabling the FC storage protocol. The Rapid Cloning Utility (RCU) handles all LUN creation, masking, and other options.

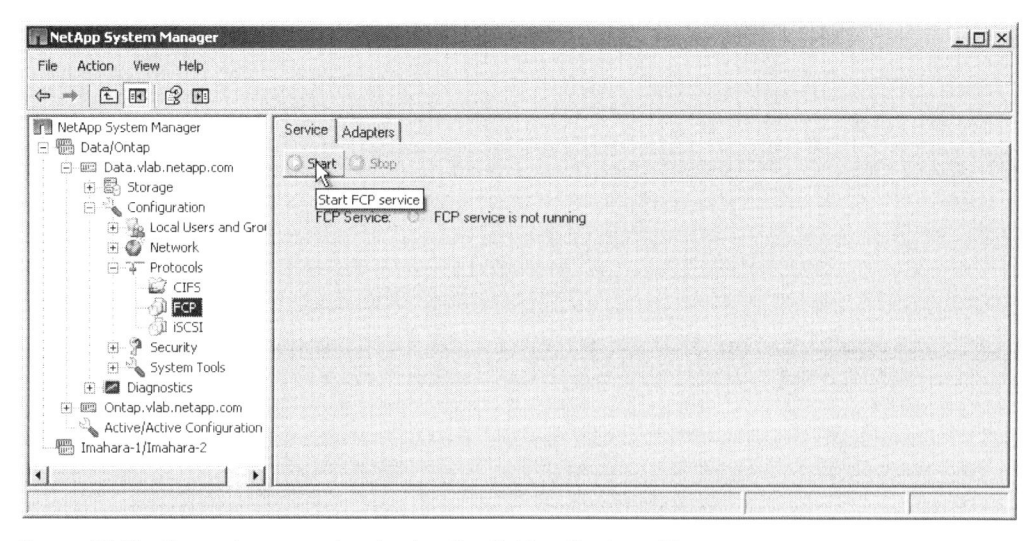

Figure 48) Starting a storage protocol using the NetApp Systems Manager.

If your plans are to deploy with IP-based storage access, NFS, or iSCSI, then you need to configure multiple Ethernet links to operate together as an EtherChannel. The determining factor of how your network ports are configured is based on the capabilities of your network switches. Details around these capabilities and completing the network port configuration process are covered in section 3.

MONITORING STORAGE USE WITH NETAPP SYSTEMS MANAGER

NetApp Systems Manager can monitor, manage, and generate reports on current generation NetApp FAS systems in small to medium size organizations.

When using storage savings technologies, such as thin provisioning and deduplication, it is very important to monitor the free space available in storage aggregates. Proper notification of the available free space means that additional storage can be made available before the aggregate becomes completely full.

NetApp recommends setting up e-mail and pager notifications to the appropriate administrators and SNMP monitoring. These can both be configured in the NSM.

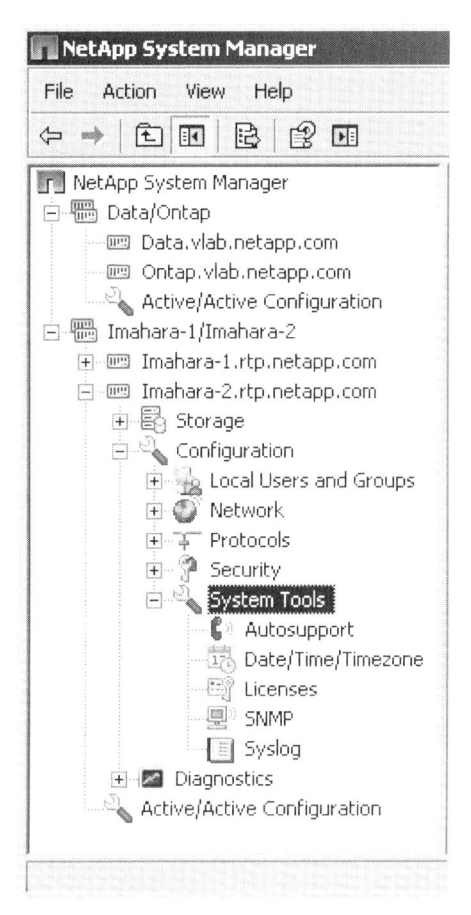

Figure 49) Setting up monitoring in the NetApp Systems Manager.

MONITORING STORAGE USE WITH NETAPP OPERATIONS MANAGER

NetApp Operations Manager monitors, manages, and generates reports on all of the NetApp FAS systems in medium to large size organizations. When you are using NetApp thin provisioning, NetApp recommends deploying Operations Manager and setting up e-mail and pager notifications to the appropriate administrators. With thin-provisioned storage, it is very important to monitor the free space available in storage aggregates. Proper notification of the available free space means that additional storage can be made available before the aggregate becomes completely full. For more information about setting up notifications see DataFabric Manager Server: Operations Manager Administration Guide.

4.5 CREATING A SERVICE ACCOUNT FOR THE CORE FEATURE OF THE VIRTUAL STORAGE CONSOLE 2.0

While you can use the NetApp root user account as the VSC service account, it is typically not a recommended practice. In this section we will cover how to create a user account within Data ONTAP for use as the service account within the VSC. This account is granted only the rights required to enable the functionality of the VSC 2.0 core features using NetApp role-based access controls (RBACs) on the storage array.

Note that this section describes only the RBAC rights necessary to enable the VSC core features in the VSC 2.0 framework.

ARRAY-SIDE CONFIGURATION

The first part of enabling RBAC is to create a new user, group, and role where the group contains the user and has the role assigned to it. In order to complete this process you, need to execute the following steps using the Data ONTAP command line interface (SSH, console connection, or telnet).

Note: Copying and pasting commands from this document might result in incorrectly transferred characters cause by end-of-line breaks or carriage returns. Such errors cause the commands to fail. It's recommended that you copy and paste the given commands into a text editor prior to entering on the array so the characters can be verified and corrected before being pasted into the NetApp CLI console.

STEP 1: CREATE A ROLE DEFINING THE RIGHTS REQUIRED FOR VSC CORE FEATURES

Enter the following command on each storage controller. You need to create a name for this role.

```
useradmin role add "role_name" -a login-http-admin,api-aggr-list-
info,api-cf-get-partner,api-cf-status,api-disk-list-info,api-ems-
autosupport-log,api-fcp-adapter-list-info,api-fcp-get-cfmode,api-
license-list-info,api-lun-get-vdisk-attributes,api-lun-list info,api-
lun-map-list-info,api-nfs exportfs-list-rules,api-qtree-list,api-snmp-
get,api-snmp-get-next,api-system-get-info,api-system-get-version,api-
volume-autosize-get,api-volume-list-info,api-volume-options-list-info
```

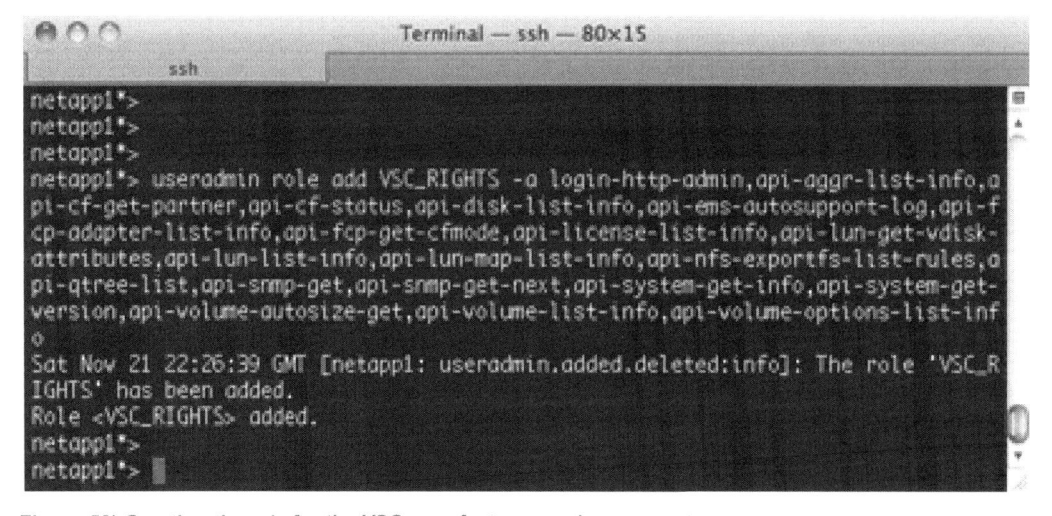

Figure 50) Creating the role for the VSC core feature service account.

STEP 2: CREATE A USER GROUP AND ASSIGN THE ROLE TO THE GROUP

Enter the following command on each storage controller. You need to create a name for this group and reference the role name created in the previous step.

useradmin group add "group_name" -r "role_name"

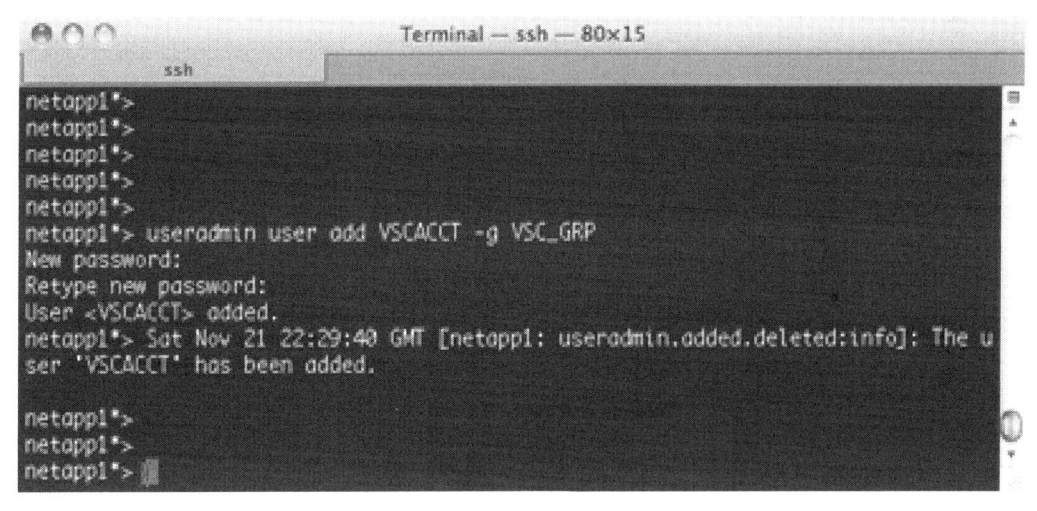

Figure 51) Creating the group for the VSC core feature service account.

STEP 3: CREATE A USER ACCOUNT IN THE GROUP THAT WILL BE USED BY THE VSC

Enter the following command on each storage controller. You need to create a name and password for this user account and reference the group name created in the previous step.

```
useradmin user add "user_name" -g "group_name"
```

Note: You will be prompted to create the account password.

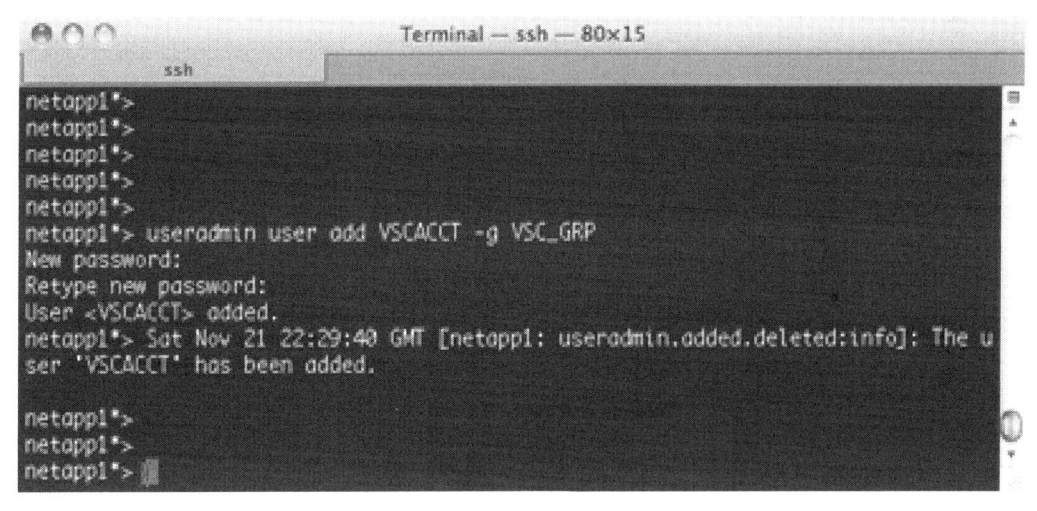

Figure 52) Creating the user for the VSC core feature service account.

STEP 4: VERIFY YOUR WORK

Enter the following command on each storage controller. You need to reference the user account created in the previous step.

```
useradmin user list "user_name"
```

The user and group information is displayed and should match the entries in the previous three steps.

```
netapp1*> useradmin user list VSCACCT
Name: VSCACCT
Info:
Rid: 131075
Groups: VSC_GRP
Full Name:
Allowed Capabilities: login-http-admin,api-aggr-list-info,api-cf-get-partner,api
-cf-status,api-disk-list-info,api-ems-autosupport-log,api-fcp-adapter-list-info,
api-fcp-get-cfmode,api-license-list-info,api-lun-get-vdisk-attributes,api-lun-li
st-info,api-lun-map-list-info,api-nfs-exportfs-list-rules,api-qtree-list,api-snm
p-get,api-snmp-get-next,api-system-get-info,api-system-get-version,api-volume-au
tosize-get,api-volume-list-info,api-volume-options-list-info
Password min/max age in days: 0/4294967295
Status: enabled
```

Figure 53) Verifying the creation of the VSC core feature service account.

Use this restricted service account with the VSC during the installation phase.

4.6 SETTING STORAGE MANAGEMENT OPTIONS FOR THE PROVISIONING AND CLONING FEATURE OF THE VSC 2.0

The ability to provision storage resources to the VI admin team can enable a very dynamic infrastructure, which greatly simplifies storage operations and accelerates the virtualization of the data center. This new model doesn't have to be an all-or-nothing enablement as the functionality of the Rapid Cloning Utility can be restricted to one of four roles.

Today these roles are global to the functionality available to all administrators in vCenter. A future update enables these roles to be assigned to individual vCenter users or groups.

THE AVAILABLE ROLES

The Provisioning and Cloning feature of the VSC 2.0 enables the storage administrator to delegate capabilities to the virtual administrator in such a way as to create one of the four roles listed in Figure 54. Each role builds upon the functionality available to lower role(s). The more RBAC rights enabled for the virtual administrator, the more functionality is enabled in VSC.

Destroy Datastores: Disconnects and deletes

Modify Datastores: Resize & dedupe

Create Datastores: Provision SAN & NAS

Create Clones: Pre-deduplicated VMs

Figure 54) The four provisioning and cloning roles available to the VSC.

These roles are enabled by creating a service account on the storage array that is entered as the service account in the Provisioning and Cloning interface. This account can be modified at any time on the storage array, and these changes will become apparent in vCenter. This enables the storage administrative team to have root control of the array while enabling the VMware team to manage its storage resource pools.

For entering this account in the VSC, see section 5.3.

In order to create this account, complete the following steps:

STEP 1: CREATE THE REQUIRED PROVISIONING AND CLONING ROLE

In this section we will carry out the basic role of creating clones. This role is the basic role required by the VSC for basic Provisioning and Cloning functionality. This role is created on the array and is required for higher level functionality by the VSC. Enter the following command on each storage controller. For examples of creating roles, see section 4.5.

```
useradmin role add create_clones -a login-http-admin,api-system-get-
version,api-system-get-info,api-system-cli,api-license-list-info,cli-
ifconfig,api-aggr-list-info,api-volume-list-info,api-lun-list-info,api-
lun-map-list-info,api-igroup-list-info,api-ems-autosupport-log,api-file-
get-file-info,api-clone-*,api-file-create-directory,api-file-read-
file,api-file-delete-file,api-file-write-file,cli-mv,api-file-delete-
directory,cli-ndmpd,cli-ndmpcopy,api-useradmin-user-list,api-cf-
status,api-snapshot-list-info,api-volume-autosize-get,api-iscsi-session-
list-info,api-iscsi-portal-list-info,api-fcp-service-status,api-iscsi-
service-status,cli-df,api-snapmirror-get-volume-status,api-quota-
report,api-qtree-list,api-system-api-list,api-vfiler-list-info
```

STEP 2: ADD ADDITIONAL OPTIONAL ROLES

In this section we will create three additional roles on the array, and we will assign the Provisioning and Cloning user account used by the VSC to the desired role. Enter the following command on each storage controller. For examples of creating roles, see section 4.5.

```
useradmin role add create_datastores -a api-volume-create,api-volume-
set-option,api-volume-autosize-set,api-sis-enable,api-sis-start,api-
snapshot-create,api-snapshot-set-reserve,api-volume-clone-create,api-
nfs-exportfs-list-rules-2,api-nfs-exportfs-modify-rule-2,api-nfs-
exportfs-load-exports,api-igroup-create,api-lun-create-by-size,api-lun-
map,api-lun-set-comment,api-igroup-add,cli-qtree,cli-iscsi
```

```
useradmin role add modify_datastores -a api-volume-create,api-volume-
set-option,api-volume-autosize-set,api-sis-enable,api-sis-start,api-
snapshot-create,api-snapshot-set-reserve,api-volume-clone-create,api-
nfs-exportfs-list-rules-2,api-nfs-exportfs-modify-rule-2,api-nfs-
exportfs-load-exports,api-igroup-create,api-lun-create-by-size,api-lun-
map,api-lun-set-comment,api-igroup-add,cli-qtree,cli-iscsi ,api-volume-
size,api-sis-disable,api-sis-stop,api-lun-resize
```

```
useradmin role add destroy_datastores -a api-volume-create,api-volume-
set-option,api-volume-autosize-set,api-sis-enable,api-sis-start,api-
snapshot-create,api-snapshot-set-reserve,api-volume-clone-create,api-
nfs-exportfs-list-rules-2,api-nfs-exportfs-modify-rule-2,api-nfs-
exportfs-load-exports,api-igroup-create,api-lun-create-by-size,api-lun-
```

```
map,api-lun-set-comment,api-igroup-add,cli-qtree,cli-iscsi,api-volume-
size,api-sis-disable,api-sis-stop,api-lun-resize,api-volume-offline,api-
volume-destroy,api-lun-offline,api-lun-destroy
```

STEP 3: CREATE A USER GROUP AND ASSIGN PROVISIONING AND CLONING ROLES

Enter the following command on each the storage controller. You need to create a name for this group and reference the role name created in the previous step.

```
useradmin group add "group_name" -r "role1_name" "role2_name"
```

Remember to add the required role of create_clones and any optional roles. For examples of creating a group, see section 4.5.

STEP 4: CREATE A USER ACCOUNT IN THE GROUP FOR THE VSC

Enter the following command on each storage controller. You need to create a name and password for this user account and reference the group name created in the previous step. For examples of creating a user account, see section 4.5.

```
useradmin user add "user_name" -g "group_name"
```

Note: You will be prompted to create the account password.

STEP 5: VERIFY YOUR WORK

Enter the following command on each storage controller. You need to reference the user account created in the previous step.

```
useradmin user list "user_name"
```

The user and group information is displayed and should match the entries in the previous three steps.

Use this restricted service account as the account entered when adding storage controllers in the Provisioning and Cloning area of the VSC 2.0.

5 VSPHERE DYNAMIC STORAGE PROVISIONING AND MANAGEMENT

This section applies to:

NetApp	**Storage Administrators**
vmware	**VI Administrators**
cisco	**Network Administrators**

5.1 STORAGE PROVISIONING AND MANAGEMENT BASED ON VCENTER

As discussed earlier (see Figure 45), with the release of vSphere, NetApp has introduced a new model of storage provisioning and management that allows the virtual infrastructure administrative team to directly deploy and manipulate datastores and VMs from raw storage pools provided by the NetApp admin.

This means that this functionality is provided by the Provisioning and Cloning feature of the Virtual Storage Console 2.0 vSphere plug-in.

INTRODUCING THE NETAPP VIRTUAL STORAGE CONSOLE 2.0 VCENTER PLUG-IN

The Virtual Storage Console (VSC) 2.0 is a free product available to NetApp customers. Once installed, the VSC is accessed using the NetApp icon on the vSphere client home screen. Each of the capabilities in the VSC plug-in framework is presented as follows:

- **Virtual Storage Console**: Here the core features of the VSC prior to version 2.0 are available. These features are available free to NetApp customers.
- **Provisioning and Cloning**: This feature provides the capabilities that were previously available in the separate plug-in called the NetApp Rapid Cloning Utility (RCU). Features such as provisioning datastores and managing deduplication settings, as well as others, are available free within the tool. The rapid cloning capabilities provided by the Provisioning and Cloning feature require a NetApp FlexClone license on the storage array where clones are being created.
- **Backup and Recovery**: This feature makes available the capabilities of NetApp SnapManager for Virtual Infrastructure in the VSC 2.0 plug-in framework. This feature requires a VMware supported storage protocol, an SMVI license, and a SnapRestore® license. A SnapMirror license is required for storage-based replication, and FlexClone is required for NFS deployments.

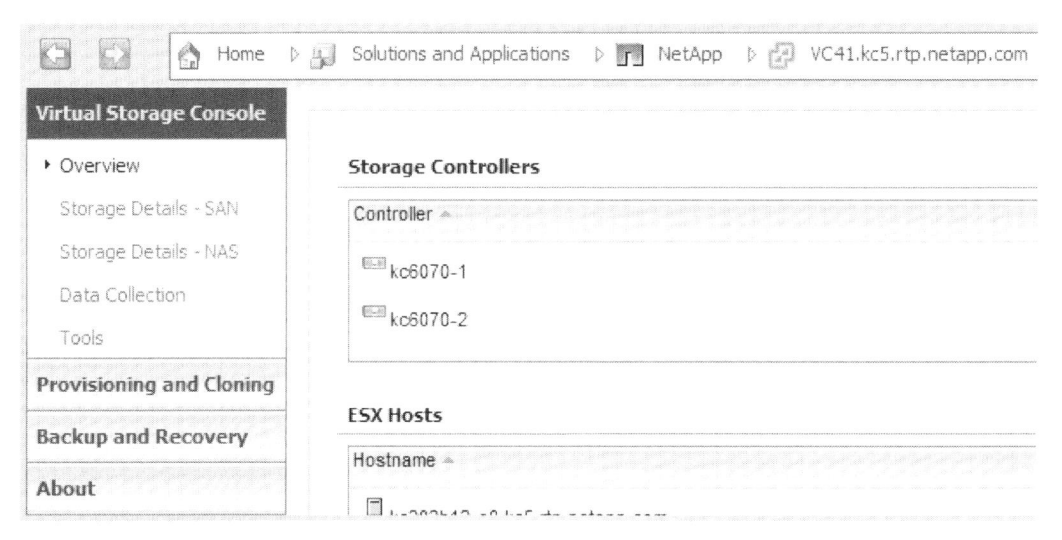

Figure 55) The Virtual Storage Console 2.0.

The core feature of the VSC makes sure of optimal availability and performance with ESX/ESXi hosts. The following is a list of the core abilities of the VSC.

- Identify and configure optimal I/O settings for FC, FCoE, iSCSI, and NFS in ESX/ESXi hosts
- Identify and configure optimal path selection policies for existing FC, FCoE, and iSCSI datastores
- Identify VAAI-capable storage arrays and if those arrays are enabled for VAAI
- Identify which ESX/ESXi hosts are connected to a particular storage array
- Monitor and report storage use at levels from the datastore to the physical disks
- Provides a central interface to collect data from storage controller, network switches, and ESX/ESXi hosts in order to aid in the resolution of I/O-related case issues.

The Provisioning and Cloning capability of the VSC provides a means to optimally provision and manage NetApp SAN and NAS datastores along with a means to provision zero-cost virtual machines directly from within vCenter. The following is a list of the Provisioning and Cloning capabilities available in the VSC 2.0.

- Delegate authority from the storage administrator to the virtual administrator for Provisioning and Cloning functions.
- Provision FC, FCoE, iSCSI, and NFS datastores.
- Automate assignment of multipathing policies to datastores with the VMware pluggable storage architecture for LUNs and ALUA-enabled LUNs and distributing NFS path connections based on a path round robin policy.
- Implement automated storage access control security when datastores are provisioned. Access control is in the form of LUN masking and NFS exports.
- Dynamically resize FC, FCoE, iSCSI, and NFS datastores on the fly.
- Provide a central interface to collect data from storage controller, network switches, and ESX/ESXi hosts in order to aid in the resolution of I/O-related case issues.

5.2 INSTALLING THE VIRTUAL STORAGE CONSOLE 2.0

The VSC provides full support for hosts running ESX/ESXi 4.0 and later and provides limited reporting functionality with hosts running ESX/ESXi 3.5 and later. Before downloading and installing the VSC, make sure that your deployment has the required components.

- A vCenter Server version 4.0 or later. The VSC can be installed on the vCenter Server or on another server or VM.
- If installing on another server or VM, this system should run 32- or 64-bit Windows Server 2008, 2003 SP1 and later, or a 32-bit version of XP Professional SP2 and later.
- Storage array is required to run Data ONTAP 7.3.1.1 or later.

For a list of supported storage adapter adapters and firmware, refer to the NetApp Interoperability Matrix.

INSTALLING THE VSC 2.0

Download the installation program to the Windows server, run the installation wizard, and follow the onscreen instructions. Once completed, this process opens a window where you register the VSC as a plug-in in vCenter Server. This final step requires a user with vCenter administrator credentials to complete the registration processes. During the installation process, you are prompted to select the features of the VSC 2.0 that will be enabled in the environment. The core Virtual Storage Console must be selected. The Provisioning and Cloning and Backup and Recovery features are the former Rapid Cloning Utility and SnapManager for Virtual Infrastructure interfaces, and certain subfeatures might require licensing, as described earlier. At a minimum NetApp recommends the installation of the Provisioning and Cloning capabilities as the procedures in this document are dependent on using these interfaces.

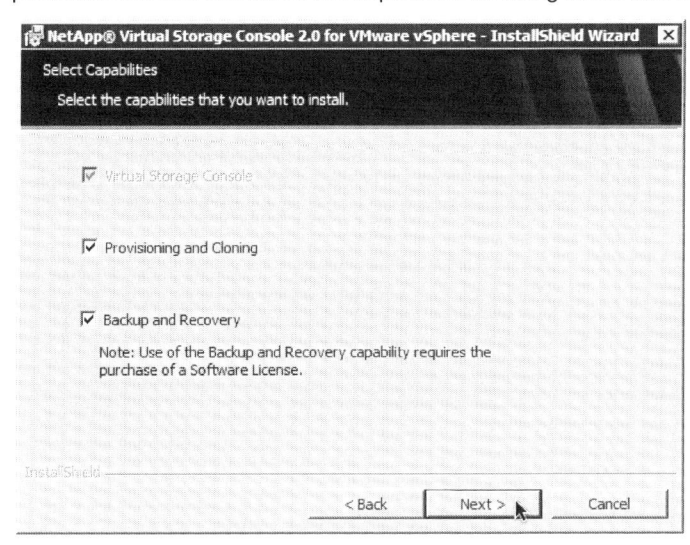

Figure 56) Selecting the VSC 2.0 features to be enabled.

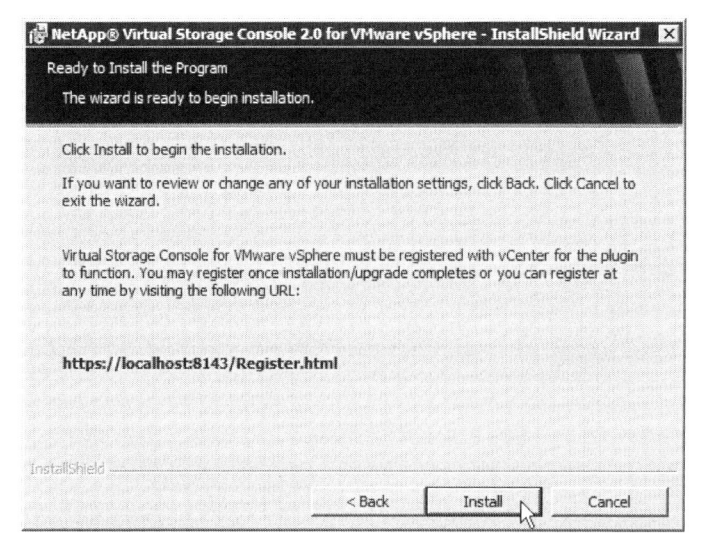

Figure 57) The install process launches the vCenter registration process.

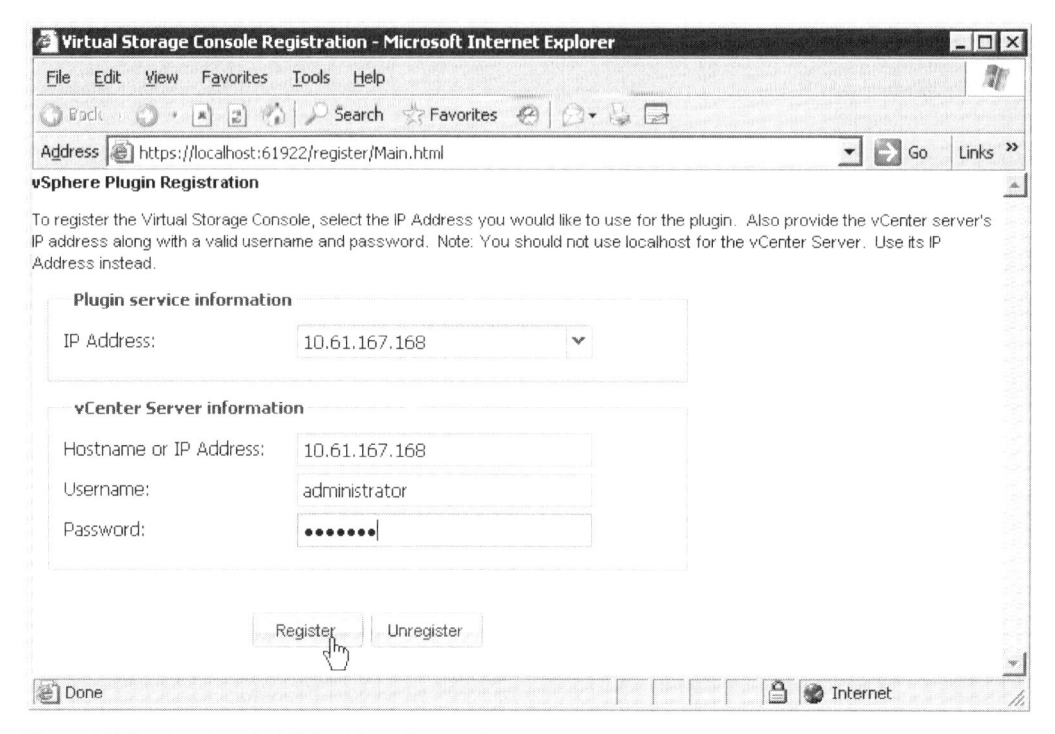

Figure 58) Registering the VSC with a vCenter Server.

5.3   ADDING STORAGE CONTROLLERS TO THE VIRTUAL STORAGE CONSOLE

Adding the storage controllers that host the virtual infrastructure to the VSC is fairly simple. Using the vSphere client, connect to vCenter, then, on the home screen, double-click the NetApp icon. Select the Virtual Storage Console tab on the left. After you have completed this step, the VSC launches and automatically identifies all storage controllers powered by Data ONTAP with storage connected to ESX/ESXi hosts in the environment. As an alternative to running discovery for the entire environment, you can select an ESX/ESXi host or cluster in the vSphere client and then select the NetApp tab in the left panel. The VSC then begins discovery of all storage controllers with storage connected to the host or cluster that was selected.

The Controller Credentials wizard starts, allowing you to enter the user or service account assigned for VSC management on the storage controller. This account can be the root account or one created for specifically for the VSC core feature, as described earlier.

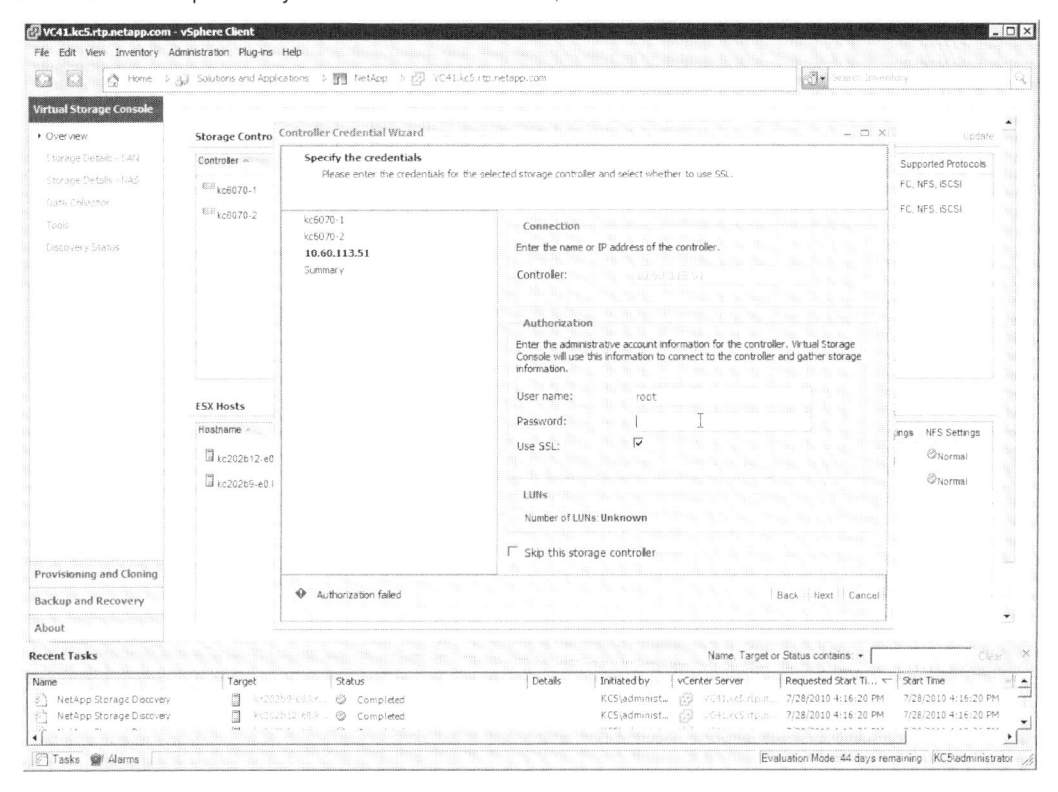

Figure 59) Adding storage controller access in the VSC.

5.4 OPTIMAL STORAGE SETTINGS FOR ESX/ESXI HOSTS

The VSC allows for the automated configuration of storage-related settings for all ESX/ESXi 4.x hosts connect to NetApp storage controllers. VMware administrators can right-click individual or multiple ESX/ESXi hosts and choose to set recommended values for these hosts. This functionality sets values for HBAs and CNAs, sets appropriate paths and path selection plug-ins, and makes sure of appropriate settings for software-based I/O (NFS and iSCSI).

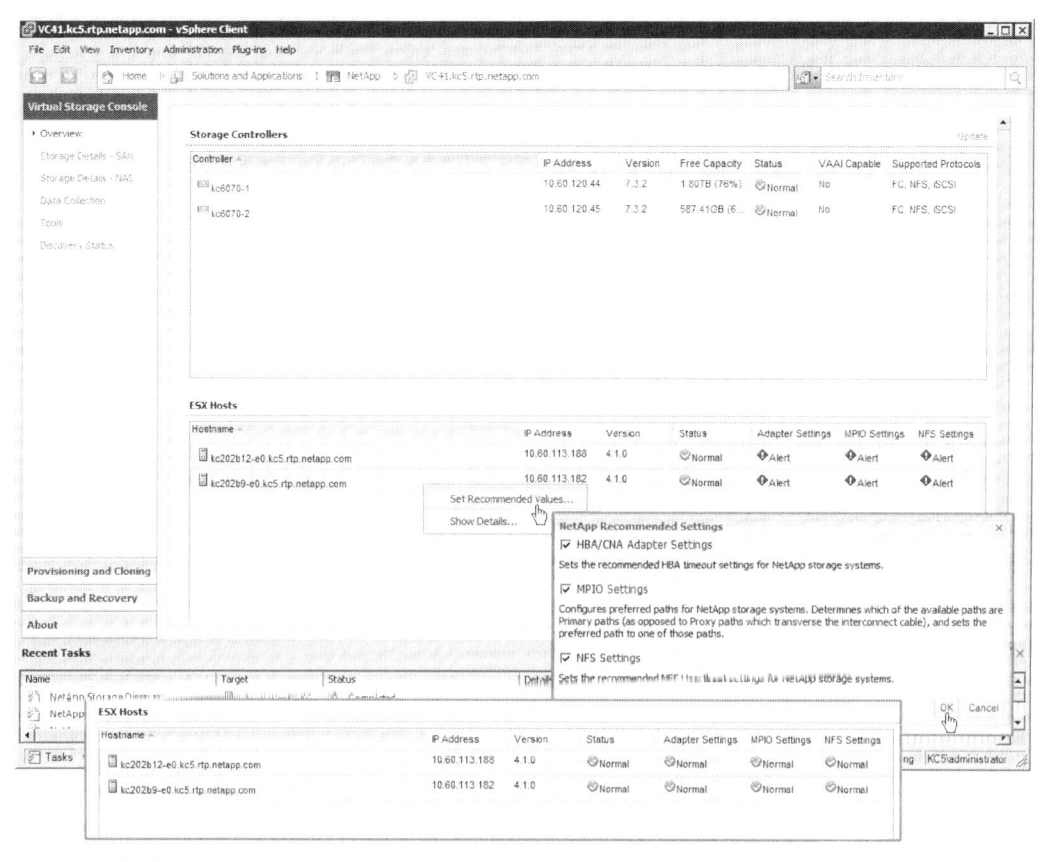

Figure 60) Setting recommended storage settings for ESX/ESXi 4.x hosts, including multipathing for existing LUNs, in the VSC.

5.5 ADDING STORAGE CONTROLLERS FOR PROVISIONING AND CLONING

The Provisioning and Cloning feature of the VSC 2.0 currently requires reauthentication of storage arrays by specifying the credentials necessary for communication. To do this using the vSphere client, connect to vCenter, select the NetApp icon on the home screen, and select the Provisioning and Cloning tab on the left. Click the Add button to begin the controller configuration wizard.

Figure 61) Launching the Provisioning and Cloning Add Controller wizard.

Select the Storage Controllers tab and select Add. This process allows you to manually add the storage controllers that you would like to use to deploy storage and clone virtual machines within vCenter. Enter the user or service account assigned on the storage controller being added. This account can be the root account or one created earlier specifically for the Provisioning and Cloning feature.

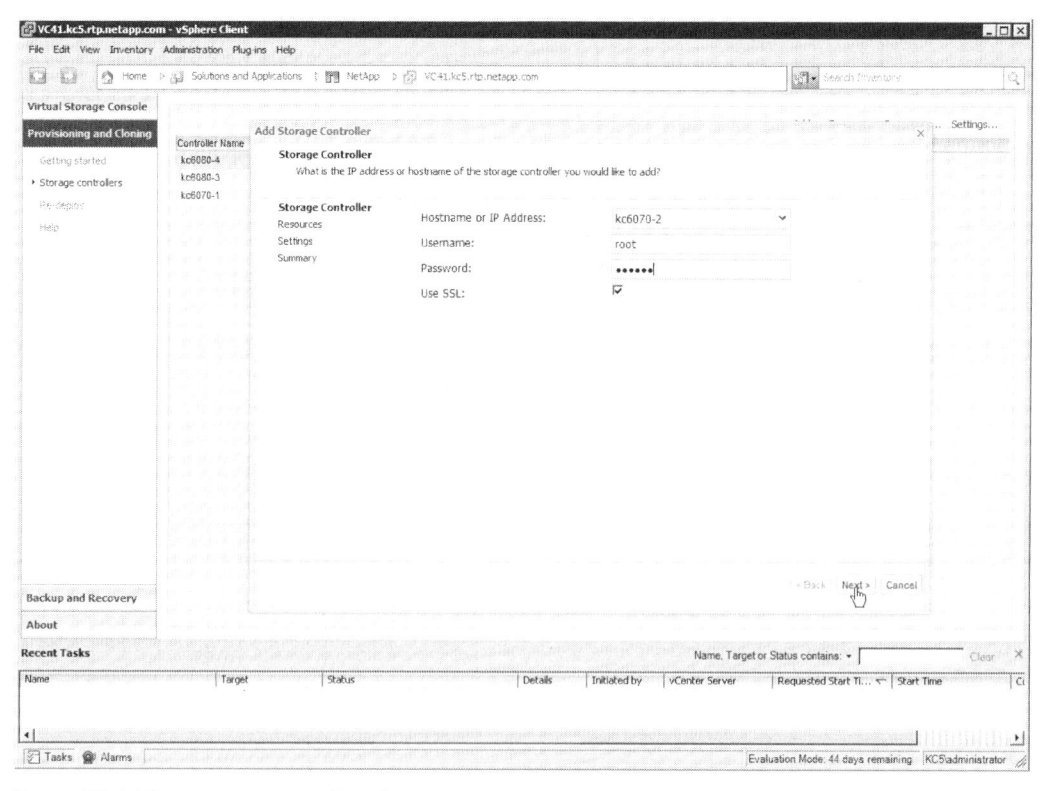

Figure 62) Adding storage controllers for management by the RCU.

5.6 ASSIGNING STORAGE RESOURCES FOR PROVISIONING AND CLONING

After the RCU is installed, the storage administrator can assign storage resources for use by the virtual infrastructure. These resources include network interfaces, FlexVol volumes (for SAN use), and aggregates (for NAS use). To assign these resources, open the Provisioning and Cloning tab in the VSC, select a controller, click the Resources button, and assign resources for use by the virtual infrastructure.

By selecting to prevent further changes (see Figure 63), the storage administrator can lock or restrict the ability to assign resources by checking this box and entering a username and password. The account used to lock these settings is created the first time this option is selected and stored securely inside the VSC.

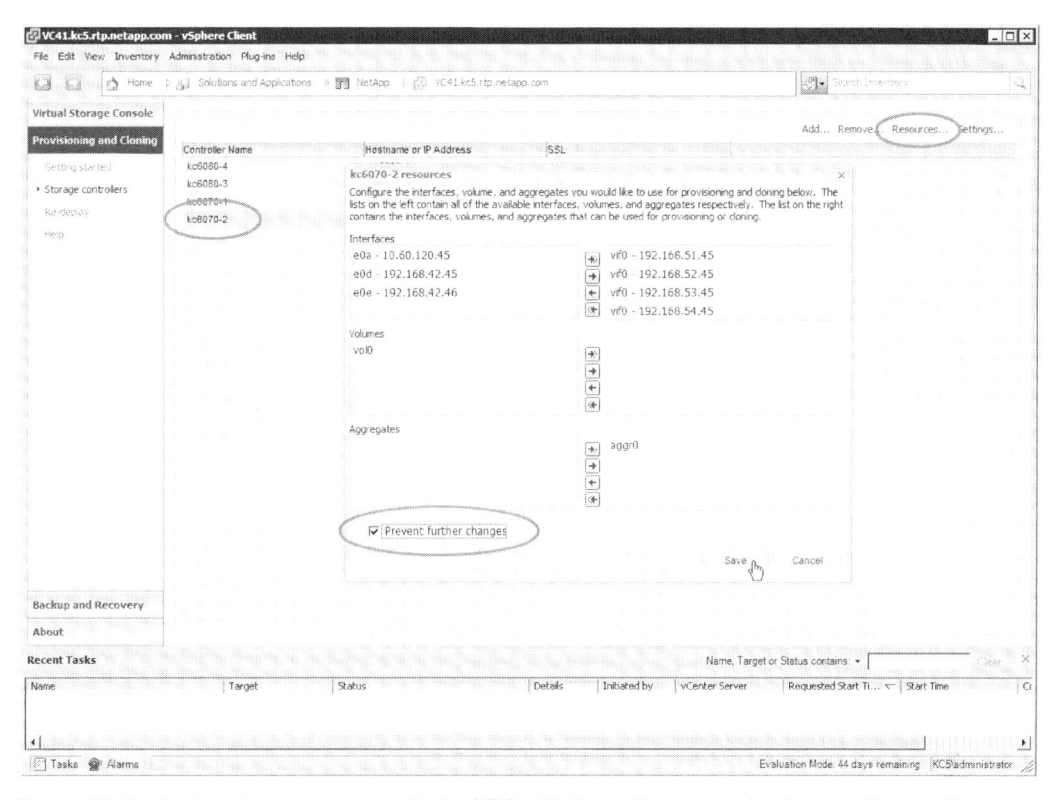

Figure 63) Assigning storage resources in the VSC with the option to restrict these settings to the storage administration team.

5.7 END-TO-END PROVISIONING OF DATASTORES IN VCENTER

After arrays and storage resources have been assigned for Provisioning and Cloning use in the VSC, VMware administrators can provision datastores from within vCenter.

The provisioning process begins by selecting and right-clicking a data center, a cluster, or an ESX/ESXi host; selecting the NetApp menu option; and clicking Provisioning and Cloning and "Provision datastore."

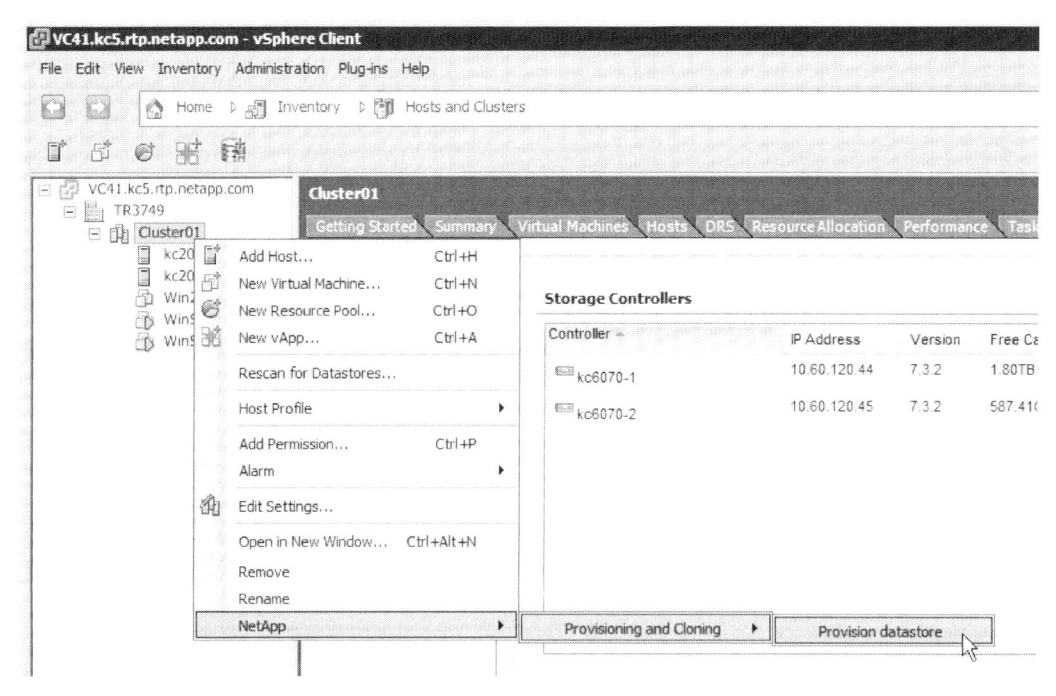

Figure 64) Starting the process to provision a new datastore on all hosts in a cluster.

This process launches the NetApp Datastore Provisioning wizard, which allows you to select the storage controller; type of datastore (VMFS or NFS); datastore details, including storage protocol and block size (if deploying a VMFS datastore); and whether the LUN should be thin provisioned. The provisioning process connects the datastore to all nodes within the selected group. For iSCSI, FC, and FCoE datastores, the VSC handles storage access control by creating initiator groups, enables ALUA, applies LUN masking, applies path selection policies, and formats the LUN with VMFS. For NFS datastores, the VSC handles storage access control by managing access rights in the exports file, and balances load across all available interfaces.

Remember, if you plan to enable data deduplication, then thin-provisioned LUNs are required in order to return storage to the free pool on the storage controller.

Figure 65 is an example of provisioning a Fibre Channel datastore named TR3749 on a thin-provisioned LUN that resides in an allocated FlexVol volume.

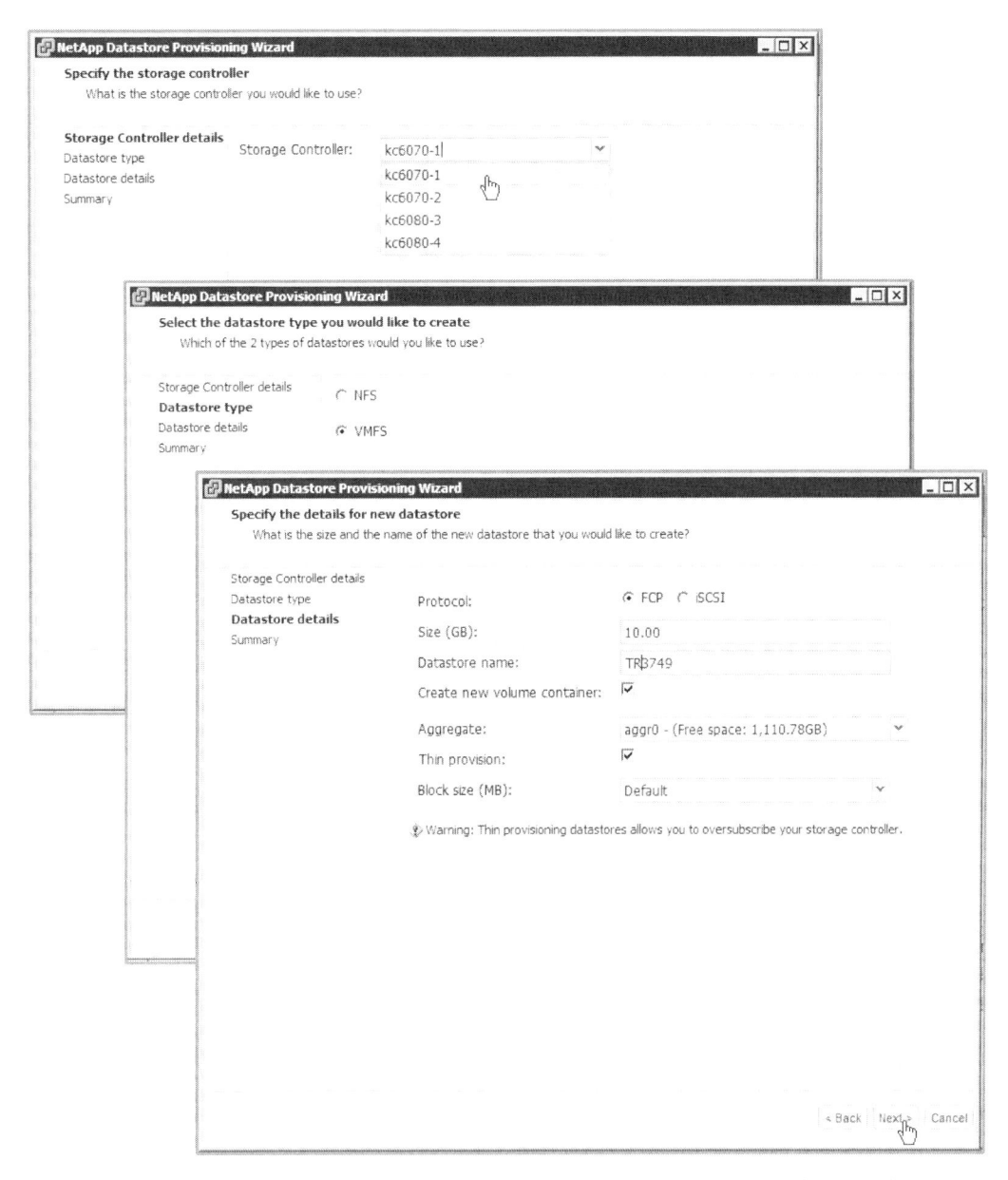

Figure 65) Provisioning a new VMFS datastore with the NetApp Datastore Provisioning wizard.

The provisioning process of NFS datastores is very similar to that of VMFS. One additional option is available to NFS datastores—they can be configured to autogrow based on datastore capacity. Figure 66 an example of provisioning an NFS datastore that is configured as thin provisioned and to autogrow.

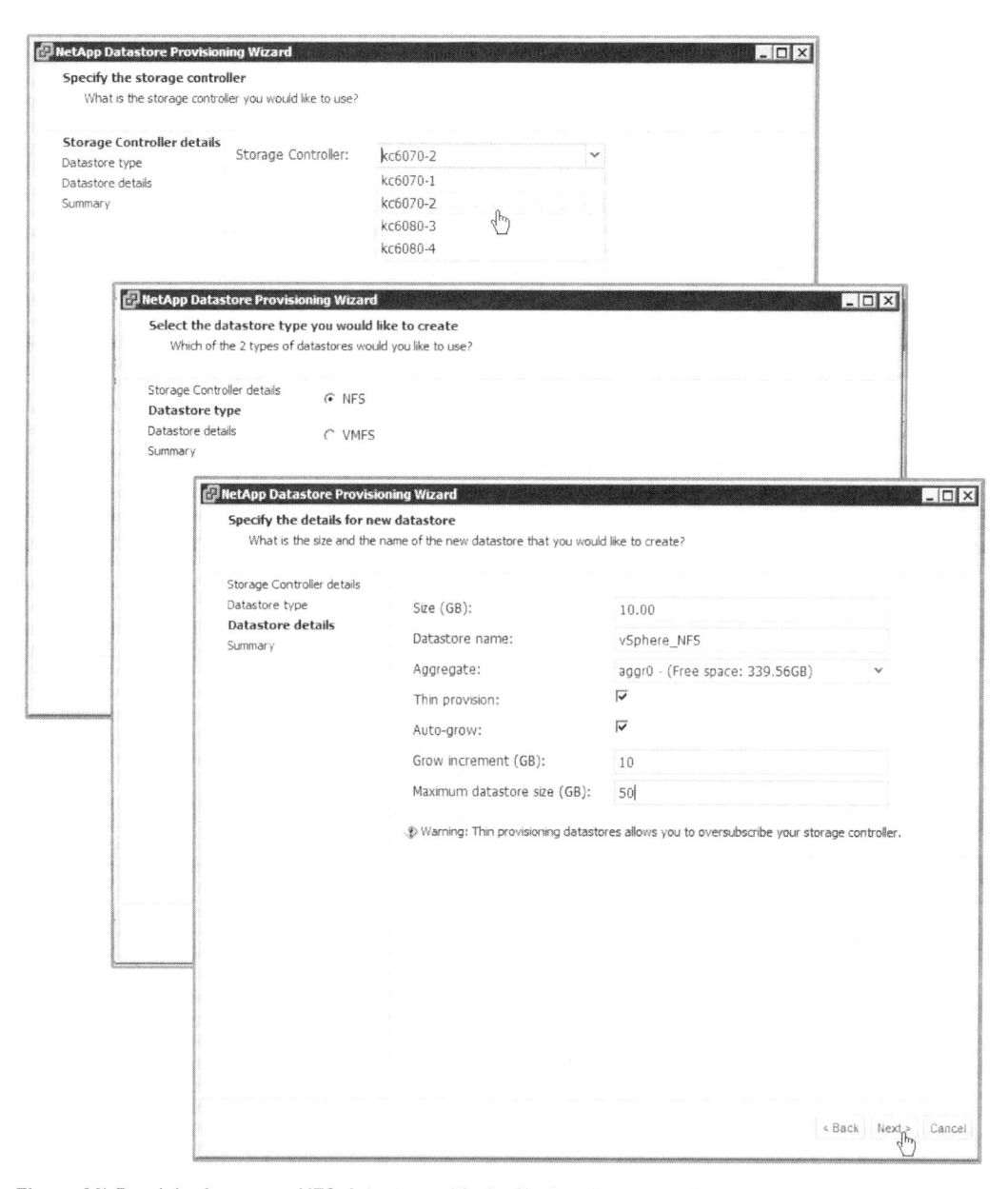

Figure 66) Provisioning a new NFS datastore with the NetApp Datastore Provisioning wizard.

5.8 CHOOSING A VIRTUAL MACHINE DATA LAYOUT

Prior to creating any storage objects, which is described in a later section, you need to determine the data layout required for your virtual machines. The following section describes common data layout scenarios. The one you implement depends on whether or not you would like to eliminate the capacity required by transient data, which could be captured in Snapshot copies or replicated over the WAN.

THE DEFAULT DATA LAYOUT

When a virtual machine is provisioned, the VMware administrator must select a datastore in which to store the files that compose the VM. The directory that is created is referred to as the VM home directory. By default, all of the files for a single VM reside in the VM home directory. The home directory includes, but is not limited to, the VM's configuration file, virtual disk and virtual disk descriptor files, VMkernel swapfile, Snapshot files, NVRAM, and so on.

From the standpoint of simplicity, this design works well where a VM home directory is a virtual machine. See Figure 67 for a high-level conceptual view of this layout.

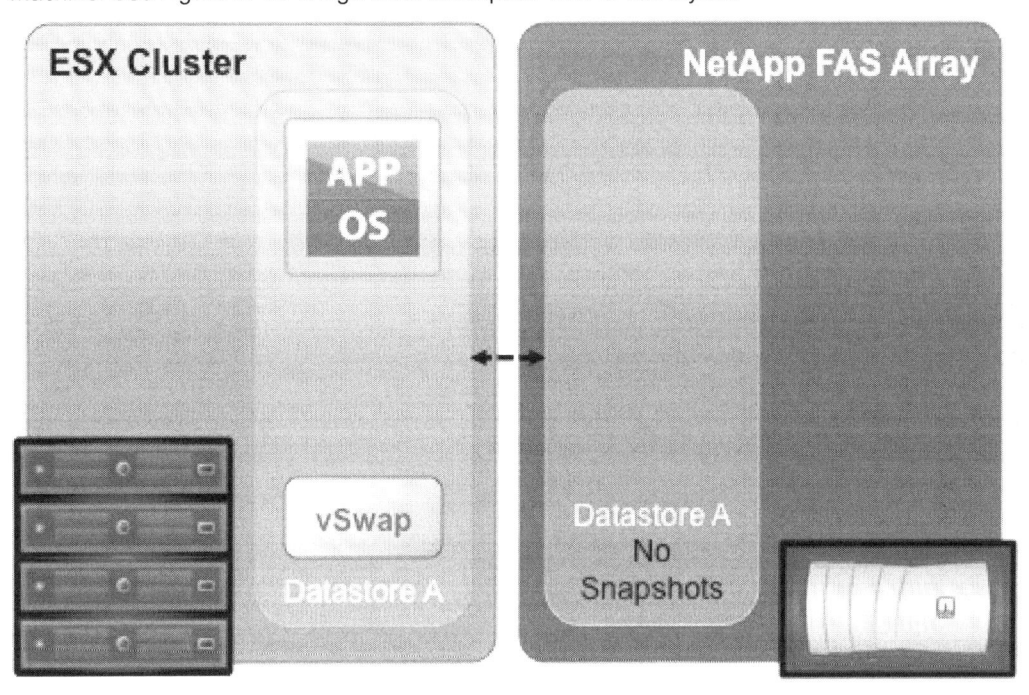

Figure 67) VMware default virtual machine and vswap layout.

VIRTUAL MACHINE LAYOUT WITH NETAPP SNAP TECHNOLOGIES

In this section we will review a data layout design that is recommended when integrating VMware with NetApp snap technologies such as SnapManager Snapshot backups or disk-to-disk replication using SnapMirror and/or SnapVault. In these use case scenarios NetApp recommends separating transient and temporary data from the production data by implementing architecture that separates these two data types into multiple datastores.

Note that this design is not NetApp specific, but instead is an optimal consideration when deploying VMware on any storage array providing Snapshot backup or disk-based replication. These types of technologies manage the files that make up a VM, not the content inside of these files, and as such, consume a substantial amount of additional disk and/or bandwidth if the temporary and transient data is not separated from the production data.

RECOMMENDED LAYOUT: IMPLEMENT A CENTRAL VMKERNEL SWAP DATASTORE

ESX servers create a VMkernel swap or vswap file for every running VM. The sizes of these files are considerable; by default the vswap is equal to the amount of memory configured for each VM. Because this data is transient in nature and not required in the case of recovering a VM from either a backup copy or using Site Recovery Manager; NetApp recommends that the VMkernel swap file for every virtual machine should be relocated from the VM home directory to a datastore on a separate NetApp volume dedicated to storing VMkernel swap files. Figure 68 shows a high-level conceptual view of this layout.

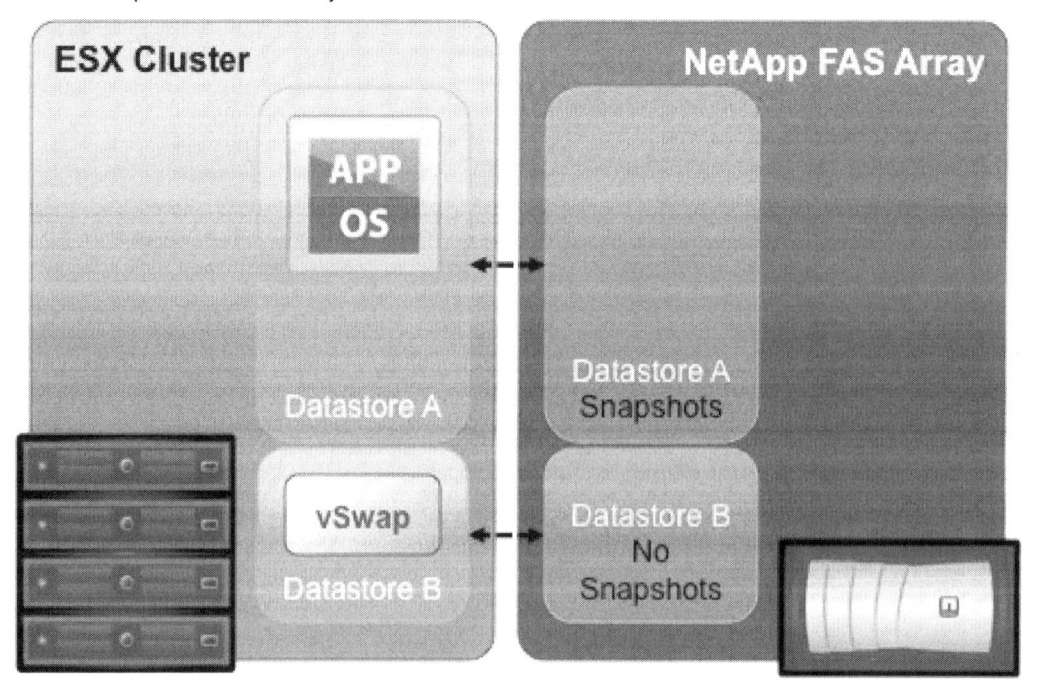

Figure 68) Recommended virtual machine layout: a central vswap datastore for the entire cluster.

A prerequisite to making this change is the creation of a datastore to store the swap files. Because the VMware swap file storage requirements are dynamic, NetApp suggests creating either a large thin-provisioned LUN or a FlexVol volume with the autogrow feature enabled. Thin-provisioned LUNs and Autogrow FlexVol volumes provide a large management benefit when storing swap files. This design removes the need to micromanage the swap space or to reduce the usage rate of the storage. Consider the alternative of storing VMware swap files on traditional storage arrays. If you undersize the swap space, the VMs fail to start; conversely, if you oversize the swap space, you have provisioned but unused storage.

The datastore that stores the vswap file is a single datastore for an entire cluster. NetApp does not recommend implementing local datastores on each ESX/ESXi host to store vswap as this configuration has a negative impact on VMotion migration times.

Figure 69 depicts the simplicity in configuring a central datastore for VMkernel swap in vCenter Server.

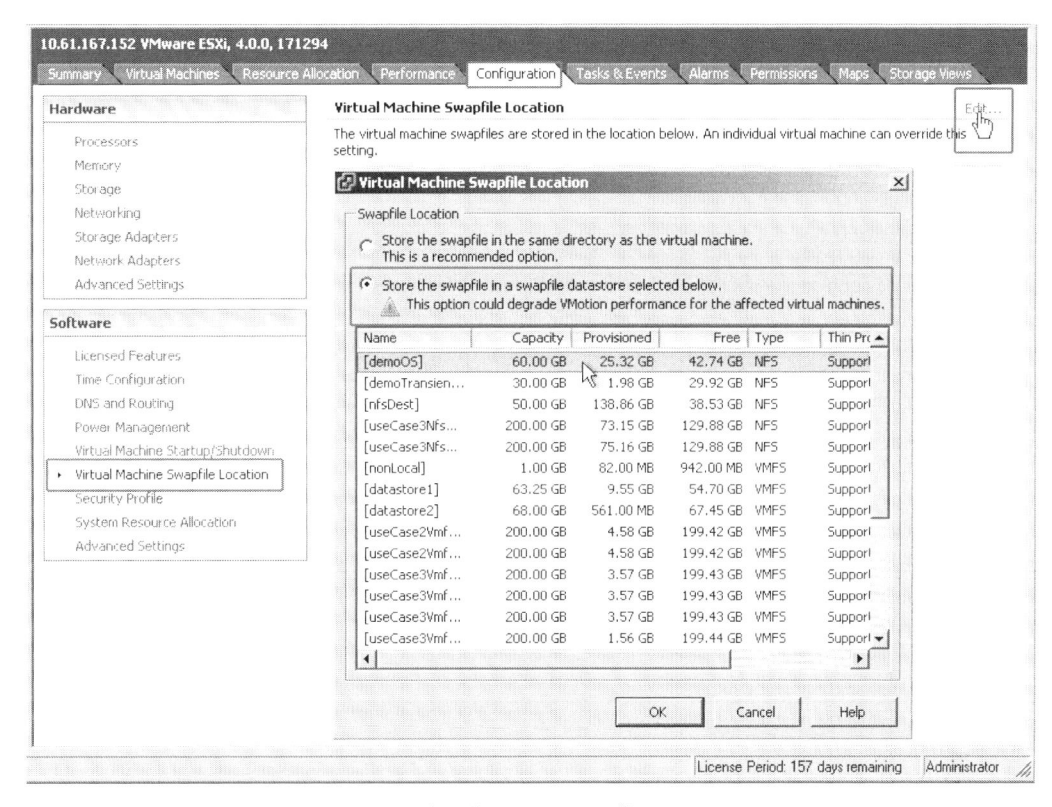

Figure 69) Configuring a central location for VMkernel swap files.

OPTIONAL LAYOUT: LOCATE VM SWAP/PAGEFILE ON A SECOND DATASTORE

This design layout builds off the layout described in the previous section, "Recommended Layout: Implement a Central vmkernel Swap Datastore." An exception is that in this design we are relocating the virtual machine's swap or pagefile in an alternative datastore. This design has pros and cons, which should be understood prior to implementing. These details are covered after we review the architecture.

Each VM creates a swap or pagefile that is typically 1.5 to 2 times the size of the amount of memory configured for each VM. Because this data is transient in nature, we can save a fair amount of storage and/or bandwidth capacity by removing this data from the datastore, which contains the production data. In order to accomplish this design, the VM's swap or pagefile must be relocated to a second virtual disk stored in a separate datastore on a separate NetApp volume. Figure 70 shows a high-level conceptual view of this layout.

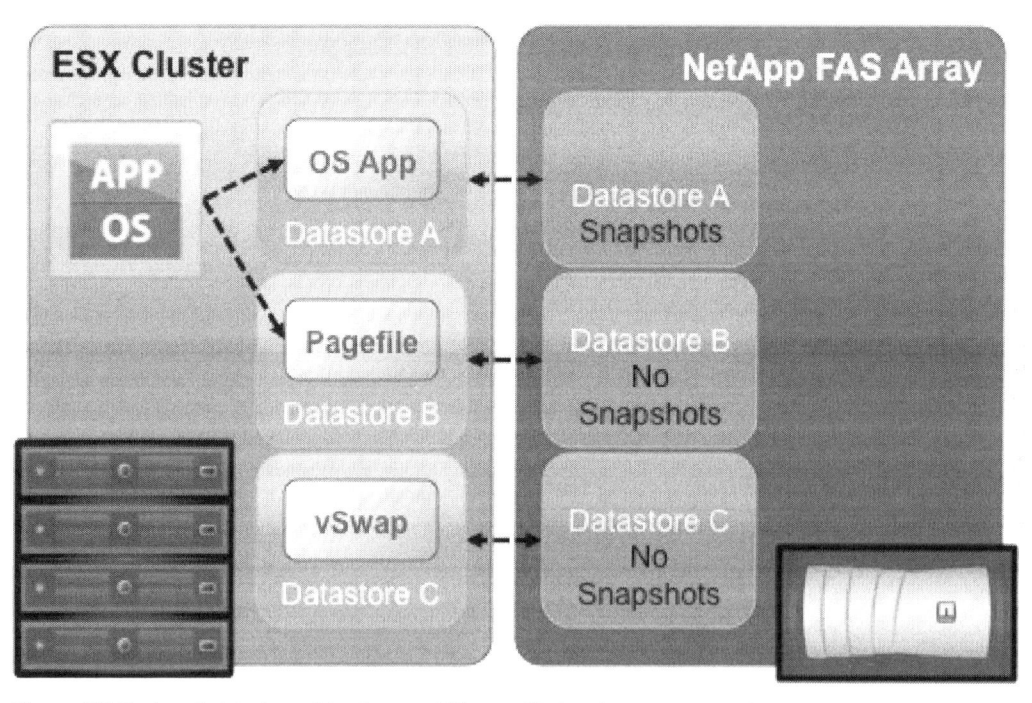

Figure 70) Optional virtual machine layout: VM pagefile has been separated to a pagefile datastore and a central vswap datastore for the entire cluster.

As stated earlier, there are pros and cons to this design. The benefit is that no temporary and transient data is contained in either a Snapshot backup or replicated dataset, thus conserving some amount of storage.

This design has an impact on customers who implement VMware vCenter Site Recovery Manager. The intent is to avoid replicating the pagefile datastore to the DR site. This design imposes some administrative overhead in that it requires an additional SRM setting be applied to each VM specifying a preexisting pagefile VMDK at the DR site in the SRM recovery plan. For more information on the details of this design with SRM, see the appendix of NetApp TR-3671: VMware vCenter Site Recovery Manager in a NetApp Environment.

5.9 RESIZING DATASTORE CAPACITY IN VCENTER

Using the VSC 2.0, the VMware administrator has the ability to dynamically resize datastores on the fly without disruption to the production environment. The VSC supports the expansion of VMFS and NFS datastores and the reduction, or shrinking, of NFS datastores. To modify the size of a datastore, simply right-click a datastore object within vCenter, then select NetApp, Provisioning and Cloning, and Resize.

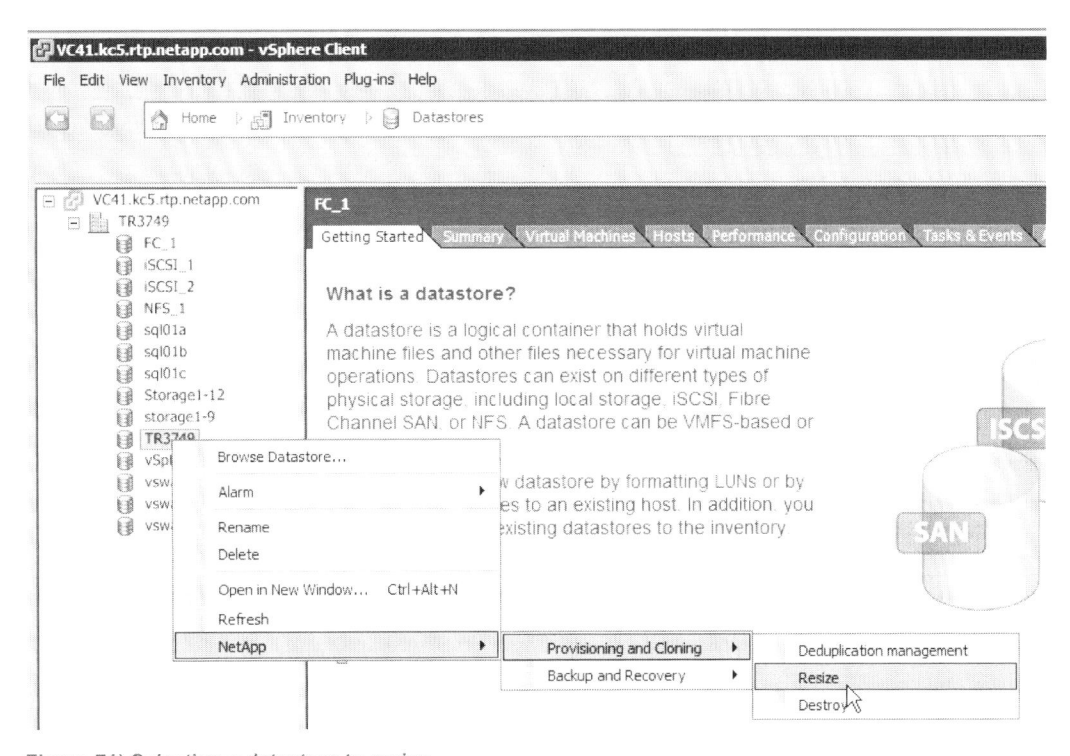

Figure 71) Selecting a datastore to resize.

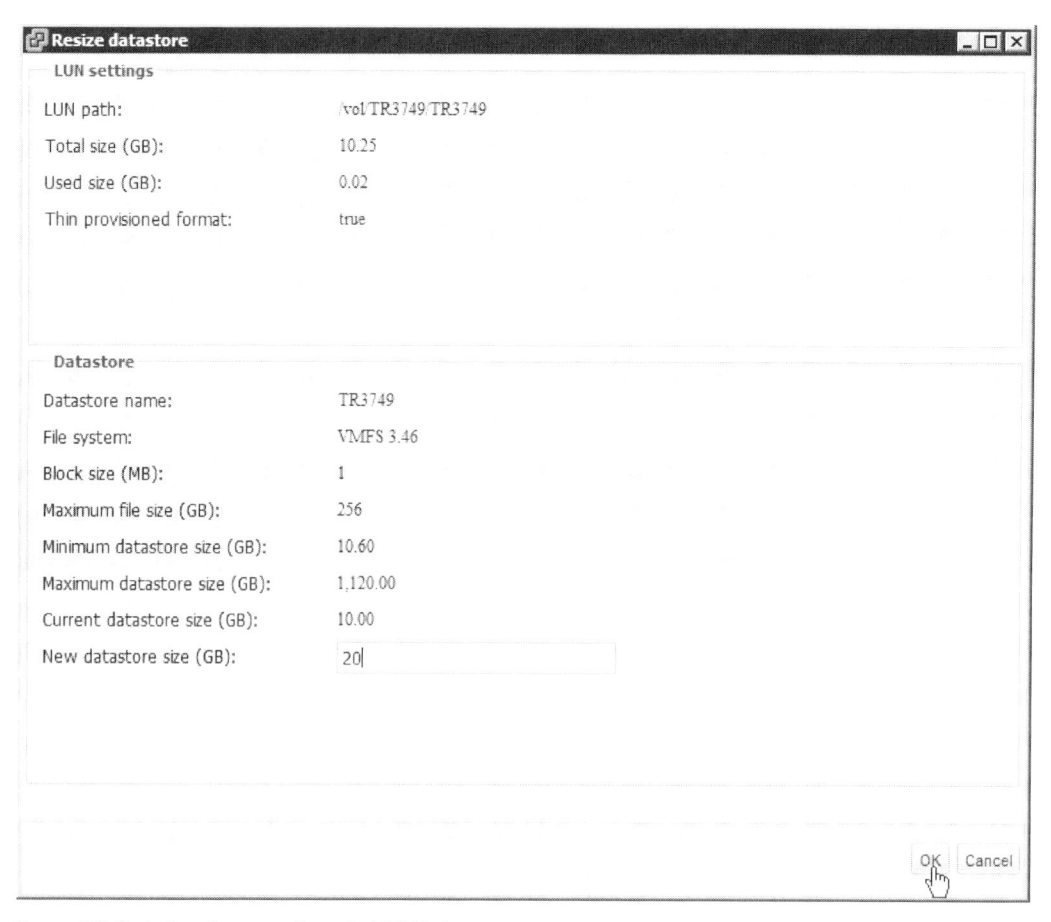

Figure 72) Entering the new size of a VMFS datastore.

5.10 MONITORING DATASTORE AND STORAGE ARRAY CAPACITY IN VCENTER

The VSC provides VMware administrators with a way to monitor storage resource usage as measured in a datastore through the various layers, including the physical disk layer. At a high level, the SAN and NAS reports appear very similar, but we should highlight a few differences and points of interest.

NFS STORAGE MONITORING

Select the NetApp tab in vCenter, and in the VSC tab select either the Storage Details-NAS or Storage Details-SAN link to view information about your datastores. By selecting an individual datastore, you are presented with additional details around the configuration of the datastore. The following sections describe a few key elements of NFS datastores.

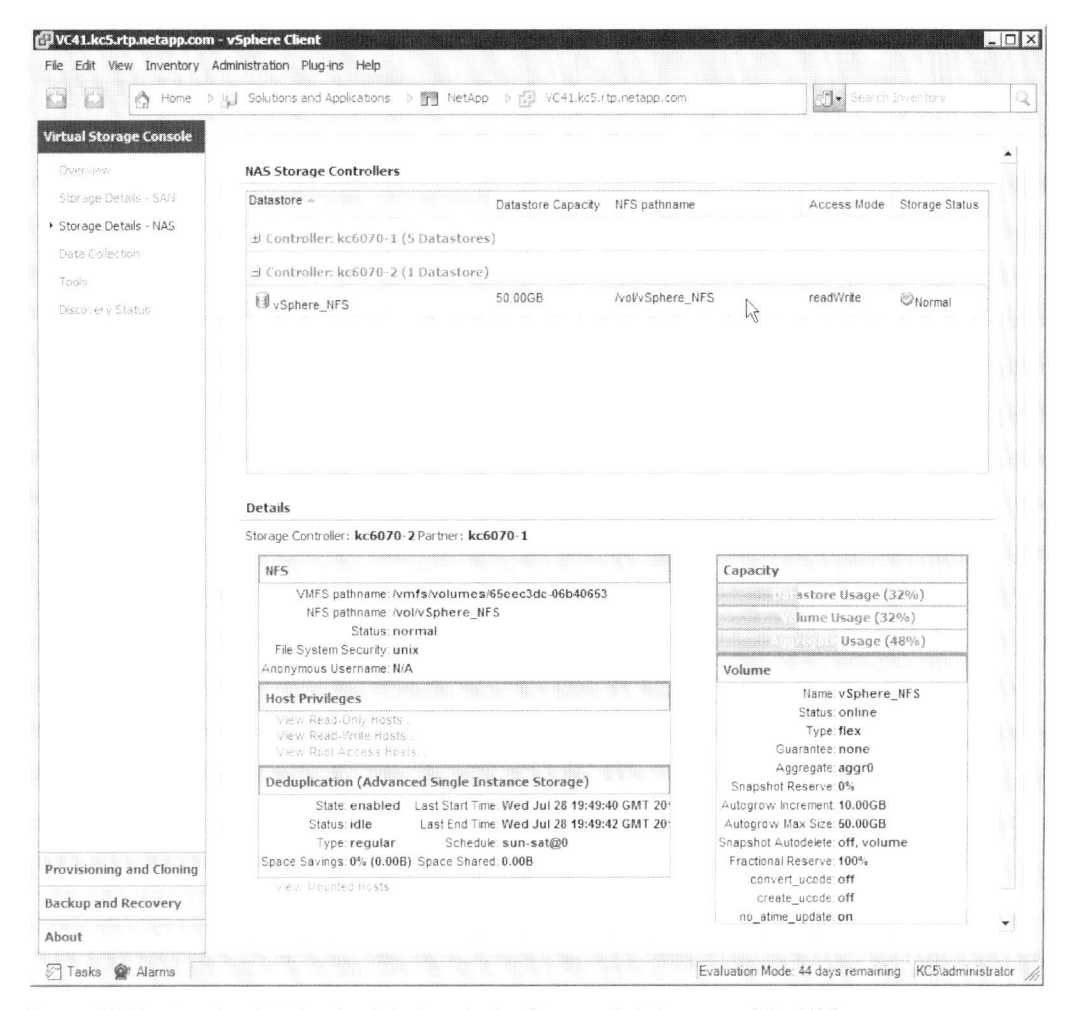

Figure 73) Viewing the details of a datastore in the Storage Details page of the VSC.

THE CAPACITY BOX

The capacity box lists the usage of the datastore, FlexVol volumes, and aggregate or physical disks. With NFS, the datastore and FlexVol volumes always display the same capacity because these are the same object. A key component to monitor is the capacity of the aggregate as it is composed of physical disk drives.

For VMFS datastores, the datastore and LUN always display the same capacity, because these are the same object. Two key components to monitor: the capacity of the FlexVol volume and the aggregate. The FlexVol volume contains the LUN, and if the LUN is thin provisioned, it is critical that the FlexVol volume be configured to autogrow in order to store the total capacity of the LUN. Should the LUN grow larger than the FlexVol volume, it results in the LUN going offline until more capacity is provided in the FlexVol volume.

You should have plans for when you near the 85% capacity of an aggregate. Options for this scenario include adding more disk drives to the aggregate or migrating either VMs or datastores to another aggregate or array.

NetApp provides NetApp Data Motion™ as a nondisruptive means to migrate entire datastores between arrays without disruption to the hosted VMs.

THE VOLUME BOX

The volume box includes some key details about the selected FlexVol volume. All of the available options are set automatically when the Provisioning and Cloning feature is used. The VSC addresses NFS datastores provisioned before the use of the VSC and updates any settings that do not match NetApp recommendations.

THE DEDUPLICATION BOX

Storage savings obtained by data deduplication are reported in the deduplication box. For NFS datastores, the space savings provided by dedupe are returned directly within the datastore for immediate use by the running VMs or for provisioning additional VMs. Dedupe savings can also be checked by right-clicking a datastore, selecting NetApp, then selecting "Deduplication management."

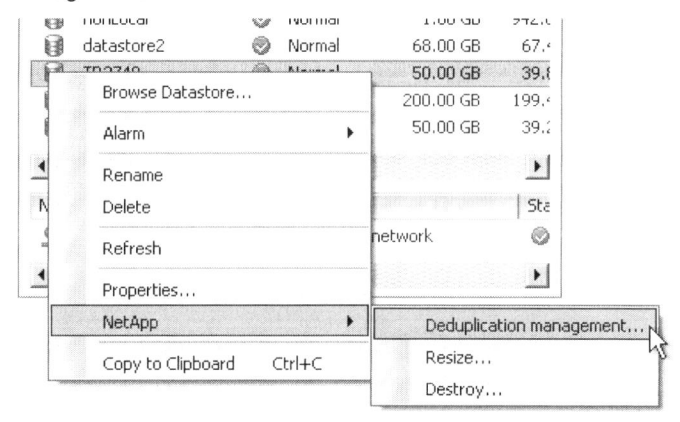

Figure 74) Viewing the details of NetApp dedupe on a datastore.

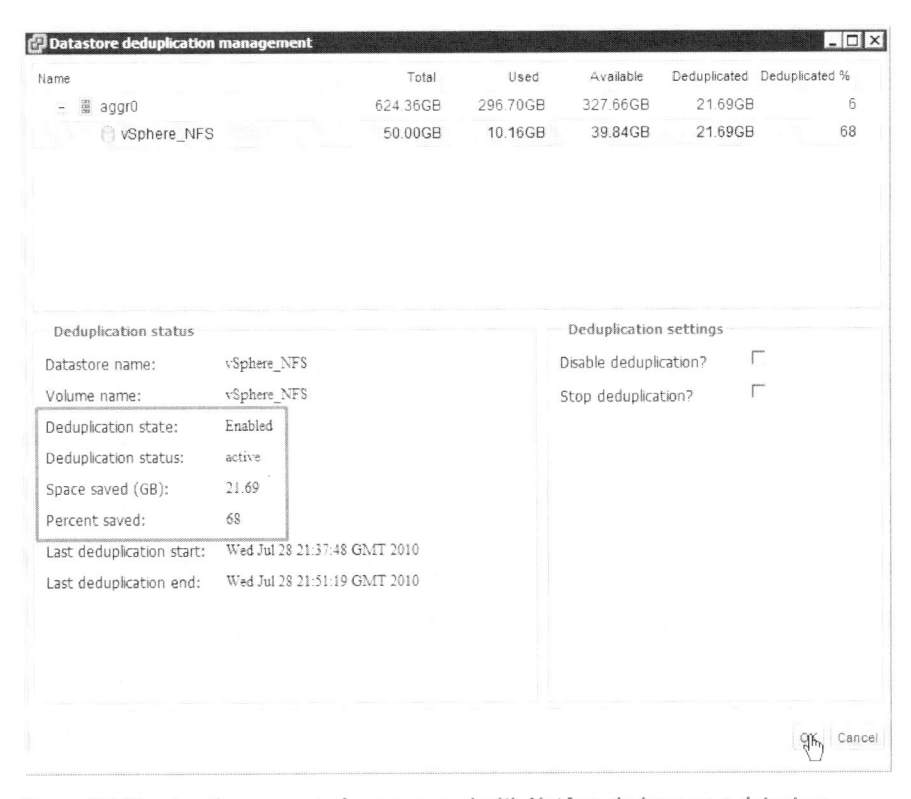

Figure 75) Viewing the amount of space saved with NetApp dedupe on a datastore.

6 VIRTUAL MACHINE CONFIGURATION AND OPTIMAL SETTINGS

This section applies to:

 Storage Administrators

VI Administrators

Virtual Machine Configuration Administrators

6.1 WINDOWS VM FILE SYSTEM PERFORMANCE

OPTIMIZING WINDOWS FILE SYSTEM FOR OPTIMAL I/O PERFORMANCE

If your virtual machine is not acting as a file server, you might want to consider implementing the following change to your virtual machines, which disables the access time updates process in NTFS. This change reduces the amount of IOPS occurring within the file system. To make this change, complete the following steps:

1. Log into a Windows VM.
2. Select Start > Run and enter `CMD`.
3. Enter `fsutil behavior set disablelastaccess 1`.

DISK DEFRAGMENTATION UTILITIES

Virtual machines stored on NetApp storage arrays should not use disk defragmentation utilities as the WAFL file system is designed to optimally place and access data at a level below the GOS file system. Should you be advised by a software vendor to run disk defragmentation utilities inside of a VM, contact the NetApp Global Support Center prior to initiating this activity.

6.2 MAKING SURE OF OPTIMUM VM AVAILABILITY

OPTIMIZING VM SCSI BUS

One of the components of the VSC, which has yet to be discussed in the document, is the GOS timeout scripts, which are a collection of ISO images that can be mounted by a VM in order to configure its local SCSI to values that are optimal for running in a virtual infrastructure.

To install the GOS timeout scripts, complete the following steps:

1. Mount the ISO image provided by the VSC.
2. From within vCenter Server, select a VM to upgrade, right-click it, and select edit settings.
3. Select CDROM and the ISO radio button.
4. Select the appropriate ISO, matching the OS of the VM you are configuring.

5. Select OK.
6. Connect to the VM console.
7. Run the script for the OS of the VM.
8. Exit and unmount the ISO image.
9. Repeat as necessary for each VM.

6.3 MAKING SURE OF OPTIMAL STORAGE PERFORMANCE

ALIGNMENT OF VM PARTITIONS AND VMFS TO STORAGE ARRAYS

Virtual machines store their data on virtual disks. As with physical disks, these virtual disks contain storage partitions and file systems, which are created by the VM's guest operating system. In order to make sure of optimal disk I/O within the VM, you must align the partitions of the virtual disks to the block boundaries of VMFS and the block boundaries of the storage array. Failure to align all three of these items results in a dramatic increase of I/O load on a storage array and negatively affects the performance of all virtual machines being served on the array.

It is the recommendation of NetApp, VMware, other storage vendors, and VMware partners that the partitions of VMs and the partitions of VMFS datastores are to be aligned to the blocks of the underlying storage array. You can find more information around VMFS and GOS file system alignment in the following documents from various vendors:

- **VMware**: Recommendations for Aligning VMFS Partitions
- **IBM**: Storage Block Alignment with VMware Virtual Infrastructure
- **EMC**: Celerra IP Storage with VMware Virtual Infrastructure
- **Dell**: Designing and Optimizing SAN Configurations
- **EMC**: CLARiiON Integration with VMware ESX server
- **Vizioncore**: vOptimizer Pro FAQ
- **Citrix, Microsoft, NetApp, and VMware**: Best Practices for File System Alignment in Virtual Environments: TR-3747

Links to all documents can be found in the section 9, "Document References."

DATASTORE ALIGNMENT

NetApp systems automate the alignment of VMFS with NetApp iSCSI, FC, and FCoE LUNs. This task is automated during the LUN provisioning phase of creating a datastore when you select the LUN type "VMware" for the LUN. Customers deploying VMware over NFS do not need to align the datastore. With any type of datastore, VMFS or NFS, the virtual disks contained within should have the partitions aligned to the blocks of the storage array.

VIRTUAL MACHINE PARTITION ALIGNMENT

When aligning the partitions of virtual disks for use with NetApp FAS systems, the starting partition offset must be divisible by 4096. As an example, the starting partition offset for Microsoft Windows 2000, 2003, and XP operating systems is 32256. This value does not align to a block size of 4096.

Virtual machines running a clean installation of Microsoft Windows 2008 or 7, or Windows Vista® operating systems automatically have their starting partitions set to 1048576. By default, this value does not require any adjustments.

Note: If your Windows 2008 or Windows Vista VMs were created by upgrading an earlier version of Microsoft Windows to one of these versions, then it is highly probable that these images require partition alignment.

6.4   MAKING SURE OF VM PARTITION ALIGNMENT

STORAGE ALIGNMENT IS CRITICAL

We would like to stress the importance of aligning the file system within the VMs to the storage array. This process should not be considered optional. Misalignment at a high level results in decreased usage.

Failure to align the file systems results in a significant increase in storage array I/O in order to meet the I/O requirements of the hosted VMs. Customers might notice this impact in virtual machines running high-performance applications, or with less than impressive storage savings with deduplication, or the need to upgrade storage array hardware.

The reason for these types of issues is misalignment results in every I/O operation executed within the VM to require multiple I/O operations on the storage array.

Simply put, you can save your company a significant amount of capital expenditures by optimizing the I/O of your VMs.

6.5   IDENTIFYING PARTITION ALIGNMENT

VERIFYING PARTITION ALIGNMENT WITH WINDOWS OPERATING SYSTEMS

To verify the starting partition offset for a virtual machine based on Windows, log onto the VM and run the system information utility (or msinfo32). There you will find the starting partition offset setting. To run msinfo32, select Start > All Programs > Accessories > System Tools > System Information (see Figure 76).

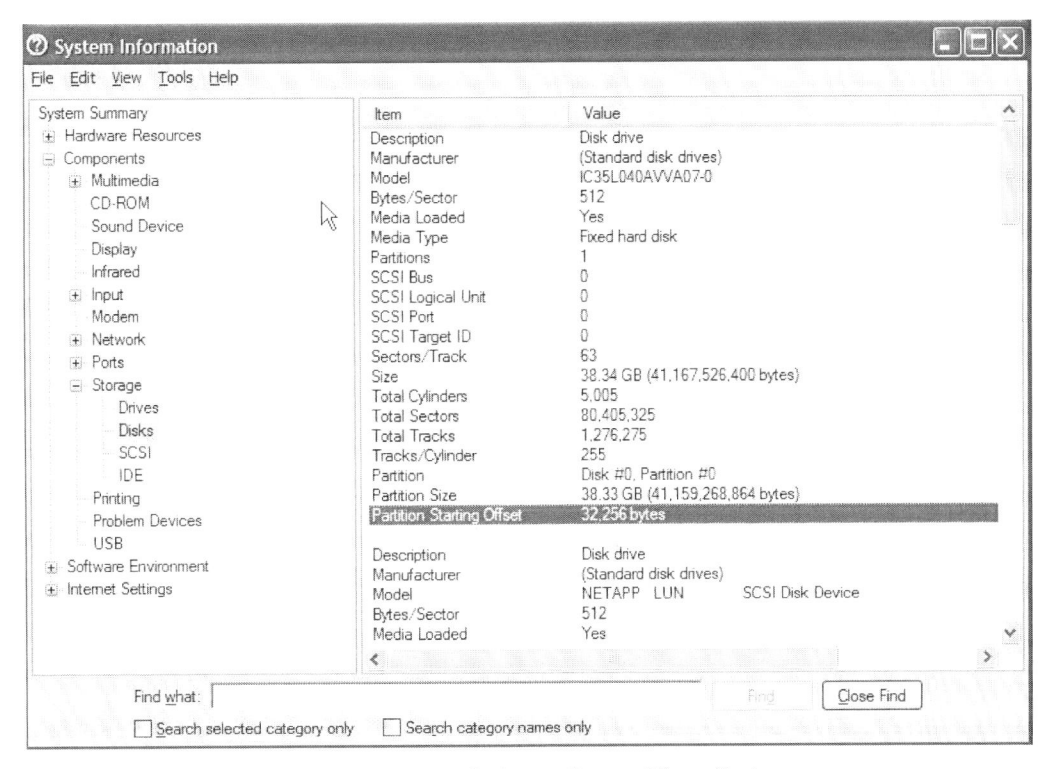

Figure 76) Using system information to identify the starting partition offset.

NETAPP MBRTOOLS: IDENTIFICATION OF PARTITION ALIGNMENT STATUS

NetApp provides a tool named MBRScan, which runs on an ESX host and can identify if partitions are aligned with Windows and Linux® virtual machines running within VMFS and NFS datastores. MBRScan is run against the virtual disk files that compose a virtual machine. While this process only requires a few seconds per VM to identify and report on the status of the partition alignment, each VM must be powered off. For this reason it might be easier to identify the file system alignment from within each VM, because this action is nondisruptive.

MBRScan is an integrated component of the VSC.

6.6   CORRECTIVE ACTIONS FOR VMS WITH MISALIGNED PARTITIONS

BEGIN BY CORRECTING THE VM TEMPLATES

After you have identified that you have misaligned partitions with your virtual machines, it is recommended that the first corrective action be to correct the partitions in your templates. This step makes sure that any newly created VM is properly aligned and does not add to the I/O load on the storage array.

CORRECTING PARTITION MISALIGNMENT WITH NETAPP MBRTOOLS

As part of the VSC tools, NetApp provides a tool named MBRAlign, which runs on an ESX host and can correct misaligned primary and secondary master boot record-based partitions. MBRAlign requires the virtual machine that is undergoing the corrective action to be powered off.

MBRAlign provides flexible repair options. For example, it can be used to migrate and align a virtual disk as well as change the format from thin to thick vmdk. It is highly recommended to create a NetApp Snapshot copy prior to executing MBRAlign. Once a VM has been corrected, powered on, and the results verified, then this Snapshot copy can be safely discarded.

MBRAlign can be obtained from the tools download link in the VSC. NetApp recommends that you contact the NetApp Global Support Center for assistance with implementing the corrective actions.

Note: Linux VMs that boot using the GRUB boot loader require the following steps after MBRAlign has been run.

1. Connect a Linux CD or CDROM ISO image to the Linux VM.
2. Boot the VM.
3. Select to boot from the CD.
4. When appropriate, execute GRUB setup to repair the boot loader.

CORRECTING PARTITION MISALIGNMENT WITH THIRD-PARTY TOOLS

NetApp endorses the use of many industry-leading third-party tools that can correct misaligned VMDKs. If you prefer a GUI tool that includes features such as job scheduling and reporting, you might want to use Vizioncore vOptimizer Pro.

6.7 CREATE PROPERLY ALIGNED PARTITIONS FOR NEW VMS

CREATING A PROPERLY ALIGNED VMDK FOR A NEW VM WITH DISKPART

Virtual disks can be formatted with the correct offset at the time of creation by simply booting the VM before installing an operating system and manually setting the partition offset. For Windows guest operating systems, consider using the Windows Preinstall Environment boot CD or alternative "live DVD" tools. To set up the starting offset, follow these steps and see Figure 77.

1. Boot the VM with the Microsoft WinPE CD.
2. Select Start > Run and enter `DISKPART`.
3. Enter Select `Disk0`.
4. Enter `Create Partition Primary Align=32`.
5. Reboot the VM with the WinPE CD.
6. Install the operating system as normal.

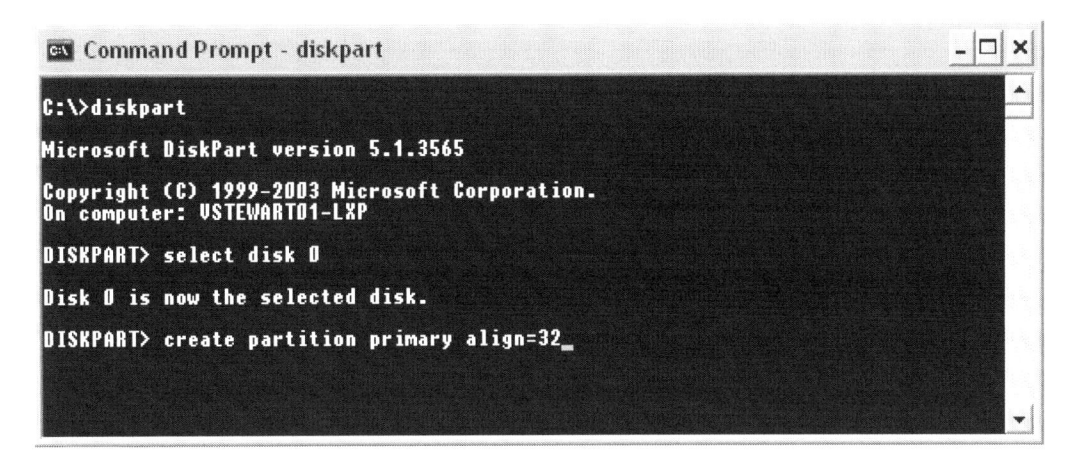

Figure 77) Running diskpart to set a proper starting partition offset.

You can also create properly aligned VMDKs with fdisk from an ESX console session. See the appendix section of this document for details.

6.8 ADDING STORAGE CAPACITY TO A VM

GROWING A VIRTUAL DISK (VMDK)

With ESX/ESXi 4 virtual disks can be extended while the VM is powered on and running. Growing the virtual disk is only half of the equation for increasing available storage; you still need to grow the file system after the VM boots. Root volumes such as C:\ in Windows and / in Linux cannot be grown dynamically or while the system is running. For these volumes, see "Growing Bootable Volumes Within a Guest Operating System," later in this report. For all other volumes, you can use native operating system tools to grow the volume. To grow a virtual disk, follow these steps:

1. Open vCenter Server.
2. Select a VM.
3. Right-click the VM and select Properties.
4. Select a virtual disk and increase its size (see Figure 78).
5. Start the VM.

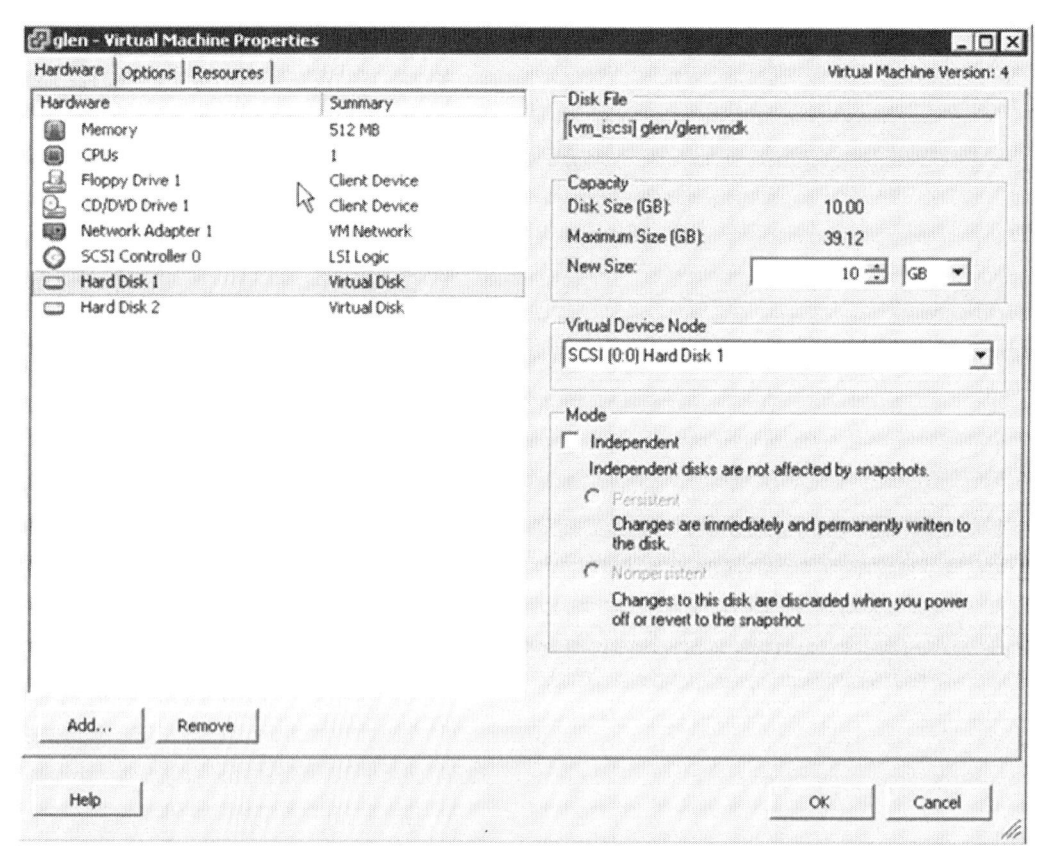

Figure 78) Increasing the size of a virtual disk.

For more information about extending a virtual disk, see the VMware ESX and ESXi Server Configuration Guide.

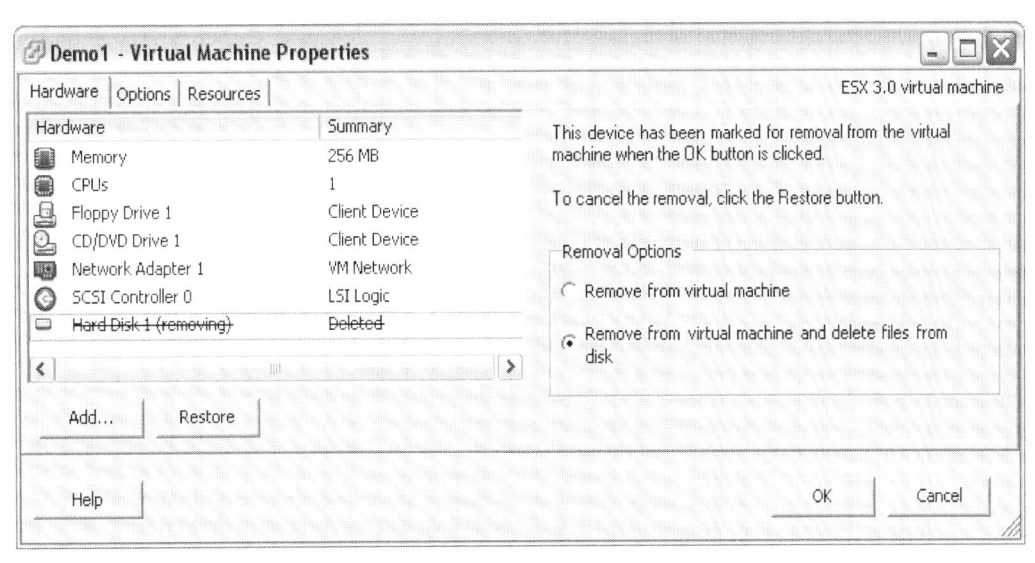

Figure 79) Deleting a VMDK from a VM.

GROWING A FILE SYSTEM WITHIN A GUEST OPERATING SYSTEM (NTFS OR EXT3)

When a virtual disk or RDM has been increased in size, you still need to grow the file system residing on it after booting the VM. This process can be done live while the system is running, by using native or freely distributed tools.

6. Remotely connect to the VM.

7. Grow the file system.

    For Windows VMs, you can use the diskpart utility to grow the file system. For more information, see http://support.microsoft.com/default.aspx?scid=kb;en-us;300415.

    Or

    For Linux VMs, you can use ext2resize to grow the file system. For more information, see http://sourceforge.net/projects/ext2resize.

In VMs running Microsoft Windows, the NetApp SnapDrive disk management software can be used to expand the size of an RDM disk from within the VM.

GROWING BOOTABLE VOLUMES WITHIN A GUEST OPERATING SYSTEM

Depending on which guest operating system you are running, the root or system volume might support live expansion. As of the time this document was written, we have confirmed that Windows 2008 supports dynamic capacity expansion. Root volumes for all other GOS such as C:\ in Windows VMs and / in Linux VMs cannot be grown on the fly or while the system is running.

There is a simple way to expand these file systems that does not require the acquisition of any additional software (except for ext2resize). This process requires the VMDK or LUN that has been resized to be connected to another virtual machine of the same operating system type using the processes defined earlier. Once the storage is connected, the hosting VM can run the utility to extend the file system. After extending the file system, this VM is shut down and the storage is disconnected. Connect the storage to the original VM. When you boot, you can verify that the boot partition now has a new size.

7 DISK-BASED SNAPSHOT BACKUPS FOR VMWARE

This section applies to:

Storage Administrators

VI Administrators

7.1 COMPLEMENTARY SNAPSHOT TECHNOLOGIES

VMware vSphere provides the ability to create Snapshot copies of virtual machines. Snapshot technologies allow the creation of point-in-time copies that provide the fastest means to recover a VM to a previous point in time. NetApp has been providing customers with the ability to create Snapshot copies of their data since 1992, and although the basic concept of a Snapshot copy is similar between NetApp and VMware, you should be aware of the differences between the two and when you should use one rather than the other.

VMware Snapshot copies provide simple point-in-time versions of VMs, allowing quick recovery. The benefit of VMware Snapshot copies is that they are easy to create and use, because they can be executed and scheduled from within vCenter Server. VMware suggests that the Snapshot technology in ESX should not be leveraged as a means to back up vSphere. For more information about native VMware Snapshot copies, including usage guidelines, see the VMware Basic System Administration Guide.

NetApp Snapshot technology can easily be integrated into VMware environments, where it provides crash-consistent versions of virtual machines for the purpose of full VM recovery, full VM cloning, or site replication and disaster recovery. This is the only Snapshot technology that does not have a negative impact on system performance.

VMware states that for optimum performance and scalability, hardware-based Snapshot technology is preferred over software-based solutions. The shortcoming of this solution is that it is not managed within vCenter Server, requiring external scripting and/or scheduling to manage the process. For details, see the VMware Basic System Administration Guide and the VMware ESX and ESXi Server Configuration Guide.

7.2 NETAPP SNAPSHOT BACKUPS FOR VSPHERE

The ability to quickly back up tens of virtual machines without impact to production operations can accelerate the adoption of VMware within an organization. NetApp offers a means to do this in the Backup and Recovery capability of the Virtual Storage Console 2.0. This feature was formerly provided in a separate interface and was called SnapManager for Virtual Infrastructure (SMVI). It builds on the NetApp SnapManager portfolio by providing array-based backups, which only consume block-level changes to each VM and can provide multiple recovery points throughout the day, and, as the backups are an integrated component within the storage array, SMVI provides recovery times that are faster than those provided by any other means.

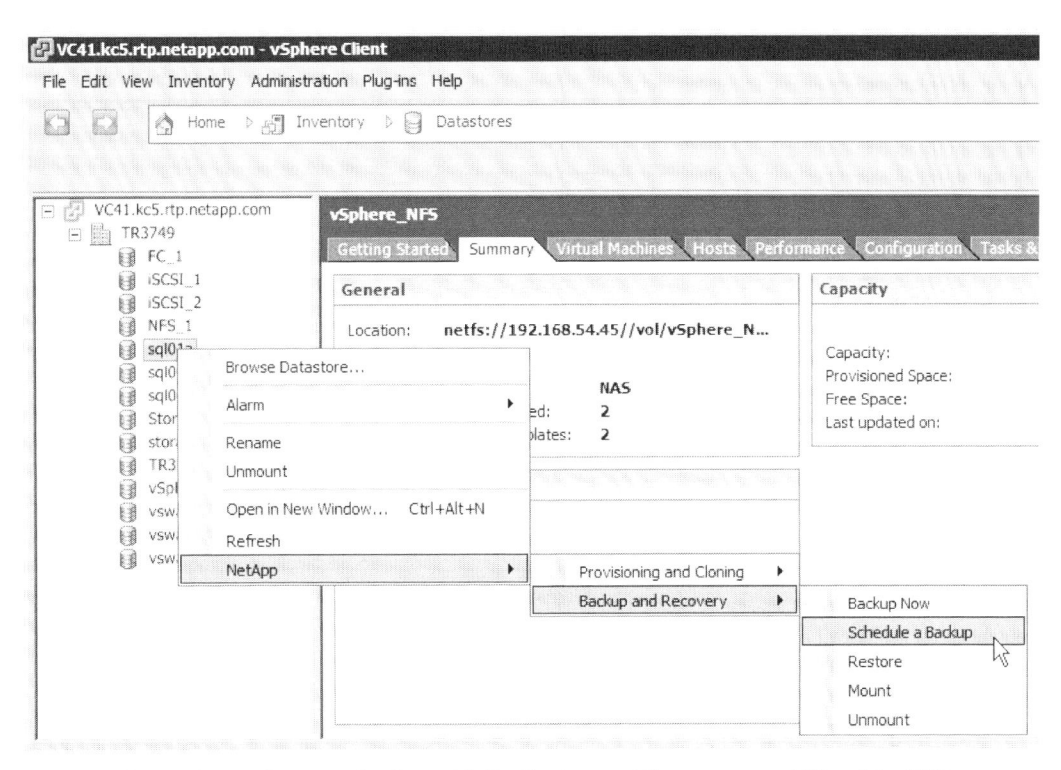

Figure 80) Scheduling a datastore backup with the Backup and Recovery capability of the VSC.

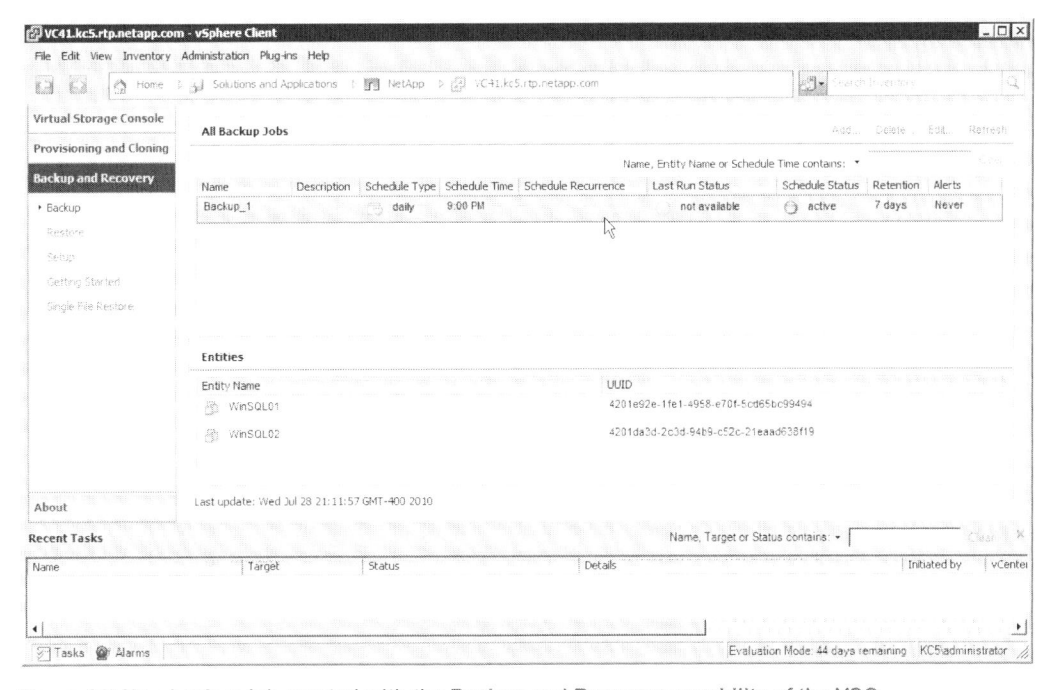

Figure 81) New backup job created with the Backup and Recovery capability of the VSC.

For information and best practices about NetApp Snapshot backups for vSphere, see TR-3737: SnapManager 2.0 for Virtual Infrastructure Best Practices.

8 TECHNICAL REPORT SUMMARY

VMware vSphere offers customers several methods of providing storage to virtual machines. All of these storage methods give customers flexibility in their infrastructure design, which in turn provides cost savings, increased storage use, and enhanced data recovery.

This technical report is not intended to be a definitive implementation or solutions guide. Expertise might be required to solve user-specific deployments. Contact your local NetApp representative to make an appointment to speak with a NetApp VMware solutions expert.

Comments about this technical report are welcome. Feel free to contact the authors by sending an e-mail to xdl-vgibutmevmtr@netapp.com; refer to TR-3749 v2.0 in the subject line of your e-mail.

9 DOCUMENT REFERENCES

VMWARE REFERENCES

- VMware Introduction to VMware vSphere
  http://vmware.com/pdf/vsphere4/r40/vsp_40_intro_vs.pdf

- ESXi Server Configuration Guides
  www.vmware.com/pdf/vsphere4/r41/vsp_41_esxi_server_config.pdf
  http://vmware.com/pdf/vsphere4/r40/vsp_40_esxi_server_config.pdf

- vSphere System Administration Guides
  www.vmware.com/pdf/vsphere4/r41/vsp_41_dc_admin_guide.pdf
  http://vmware.com/pdf/vsphere4/r40/vsp_40_admin_guide.pdf

- VMware Fibre Channel SAN Configuration Guides
  www.vmware.com/pdf/vsphere4/r41/vsp_41_san_cfg.pdf
  http://vmware.com/pdf/vsphere4/r40/vsp_40_san_cfg.pdf

- iSCSI SAN Configuration Guides
  www.vmware.com/pdf/vsphere4/r41/vsp_41_iscsi_san_cfg.pdf
  http://vmware.com/pdf/vsphere4/r40/vsp_40_iscsi_san_cfg.pdf

- vSphere Upgrade Guide
  http://vmware.com/pdf/vsphere4/r40/vsp_40_upgrade_guide.pdf

- Performance Study of VMware vStorage Thin Provisioning
  www.vmware.com/pdf/vsp_4_thinprov_perf.pdf

- All VMware documents are located at www.vmware.com/support/pubs/vs_pubs.html.

MISCELLANEOUS REFERENCES

- Total Cost Comparison: IT Decision-Maker Perspectives on EMC and NetApp Storage Solutions in Enterprise Database Environments
  www.netapp.com/library/ar/ar1038.pdf

- Wikipedia RAID Definitions and Explanations
  http://en.wikipedia.org/wiki/Redundant_array_of_independent_disks

- Microsoft Diskpart Utility
  http://support.microsoft.com/default.aspx?scid=kb;en-us;300415.

- Ext2resize
  http://sourceforge.net/projects/ext2resize.

- IBM: Storage Block Alignment with VMware Virtual Infrastructure
  ftp://service.boulder.ibm.com/storage/isv/NS3593-0.pdf

- EMC: Celerra IP Storage with VMware Virtual Infrastructure
  www.vmware.com/files/pdf/VMware_VI3_and_EMC_Celerra_IP.pdf

- Dell: Designing and Optimizing SAN Configurations
  www.dell.com/downloads/global/power/ps4q04-20040149-Mehis.pdf

- EMC: CLARiiON Integration with VMware ESX Server
  www.vmware.com/pdf/clariion_wp_eng.pdf

- Vizioncore: vOptimizer Pro FAQ
  www.vizioncore.com/products/vOptimizerPro/documents/vOptimizerProFAQ.pdf

- Cisco Nexus 1000V Series Switches Deployment Guide
  www.cisco.com/en/US/prod/collateral/switches/ps9441/ps9902/guide_c07-556626.html

NETAPP REFERENCES

- NetApp VM Insight with SANscreen
  www.netapp.com/us/products/management-software/sanscreen-vm-insight.html

- NetApp TR-3348: Block Management with Data ONTAP 7G: FlexVol, FlexClone, and Space Guarantees
  www.netapp.com/library/tr/3348.pdf

- NetApp TR-3737: SnapManager for Virtual Infrastructure Best Practices
  www.netapp.com/us/library/technical-reports/tr-3737.html

- RAID-DP: NetApp Implementation of RAID Double Parity
  http://media.netapp.com/documents/wp_3298.pdf

- NetApp TR-3671: VMware Site Recovery Manager in a NetApp Environment
  http://media.netapp.com/documents/tr-3671.pdf

- Data ONTAP File Access and Protocol Management Guide
  http://now.netapp.com/NOW/knowledge/docs/ontap/rel731/html/ontap/filesag/accessing/task/t_oc_accs_file_sharing_between_NFS_and_CIFS.html

- DataFabric Manager Server 3.7: Operations Manager Administration Guide
  http://now.netapp.com/NOW/knowledge/docs/DFM_win/rel371/html/software/opsmgr/index.htm

- NetApp: Data ONTAP File Access and Protocol Management Guide
  http://now.netapp.com/NOW/knowledge/docs/ontap/rel731/html/ontap/filesag/accessing/task/t_oc_accs_file_sharing_between_NFS_and_CIFS.html

- NetApp Systems Manager Quick Start Guide
  http://now.netapp.com/NOW/knowledge/docs/netapp_sys_mgr/rel10/html/software/qkstart/index.htm

- Setting RBAC Access with the VSC
  https://now.netapp.com/Knowledgebase/solutionarea.asp?id=kb54084

- Citrix, Microsoft, NetApp, and VMware: Best Practices for File System Alignment in Virtual Environments
  http://media.netapp.com/documents/tr-3747.pdf

- The Virtual Storage Guy Blog
  http://blogs.netapp.com/virtualstorageguy

10 VERSION HISTORY

Version	Revision Comments
1.0	May 2009 Original document
1.0.1	August 2009 Minor edits Reformatted for publishing
2.0	January 2010 Major update focusing on vCenter integrated tools for provisioning and configuration Removed all manual storage configurations to the appendix section Replaced these sections with the NSM, RCU, and VSC Reorganized the document from 16 sections to 8
2.1	August 2010 Minor edits vSphere 4.1 updates Added statement about no support for combining iSCSI multiple TCP sessions and NFS in the same hosts Removed appendixes for legacy manual processes

11 ACKNOWLEDGEMENTS

11.1 ABOUT THE AUTHORS AND CONTRIBUTORS

The authors of this technical report are members of either the NetApp Virtual Architecture Team or the Cloud Solutions Team based in Sunnyvale, California and Research Triangle Park, North Carolina.

Vaughn Stewart is the Virtualization Evangelist for NetApp and a member of the Virtualization Solutions Engineering Team. He is the coauthor of several white papers on integrating VMware technologies on NetApp systems. Vaughn is on twitter @vStewed and publishes the blog http://blogs.netapp.com/virtualstorageguy. Vaughn has a patent pending, and has earned industry certifications on technologies offered by Brocade, Cisco, IBM, Microsoft, NetApp, Sun Microsystems, and VMware. In 2009 VMware identified Vaughn as a vExpert.

Larry Touchette is a member of the Virtualization Solutions Engineering Team and has eight years of experience supporting, implementing, and designing NetApp storage, replication, and disaster recovery solutions. For the past four years Larry has been designing and implementing NetApp solutions for VMware environments and holds industry certifications from Microsoft, Sun Microsystems, and NetApp.

Michael Slisinger is a Solution Architect for NetApp's Cloud Solutions organization who has coauthored four white papers and best practice guides on integrating VMware with NetApp storage. Previously a consultant with NetApp Professional Services, Mike has over 10 years of experience with NetApp products and holds industry certifications from Microsoft and NetApp.

Peter Learmonth is a Reference Architect focused in the Virtualization Solutions Engineering Team who has been with NetApp for over nine years. Peter holds industry certifications from NetApp and VMware and has a patent pending.

Trey Layton is a Solutions Architect at Cisco who evangelizes the concepts of using Ethernet as a transport medium for mission-critical storage infrastructures leveraging technologies from Cisco's Data Center portfolio and its large ecosystem of partners and integrators. Trey has served in various engineering and leadership roles throughout the technology industry, focusing on storage, networking, and compute and virtualization infrastructure technologies. Trey currently holds industry certifications on solutions offered by Cisco, Microsoft, IBM, NetApp, and VMware.

The authors and contributors of this content have presented topics on the integration of server and storage virtualization technologies at various VMworld events. Their breakout sessions are posted online at VMworld.com.

VMWORLD 2009
- BC3189: How Storage Enhances Business Continuance: From Backup to Fault Tolerance
- TA2955: Sizing Tools for Storage in vSphere and VMware View Environments
- BC3210: Best Practices for Recovery with SRM and NFS in vSphere

VMWORLD 2008
- TA2784: Joint VMware and NetApp Best Practices for Running VI3 on IP-Based Storage
- VD2387: Storage for VDI: 1000s of Desktops for the Price of One
- TA2445: VMware over NAS: Scale, Simplify, and Save
- SP08: Enabling Virtual Storage Management Within VI3

VMWORLD 2007

- BC33: Simply Addressing the Disaster Recovery Needs of Virtual Infrastructures
- DV16: Optimizing Storage for Virtual Desktops
- IP43: Building Virtual Infrastructures with Network-Attached Storage (NAS)

www.netapp.com

Printed in Great Britain by
Amazon.co.uk, Ltd.,
Marston Gate.